Sensation of Oneness

Cooperation for Maturation,
Not Competition,
Is the Fundamental Process in Nature
And We Can Experience It as a Sensation

TERRY MOLLNER

The Love Skill Publishing

Reviews

"I've long thought that "maturation" is the key process for human societies as well as individuals--we've grown physically big enough and now we need to grow in other ways instead. Terry Mollner offers some fascinating insights into how that might be possible."

—**Bill McKibben,** Co-Founder, 350.org
author of *Falter: Has the Human Game
Begun to Play Itself Out?*

"I read through the book twice and am still going through and deepening the thoughts enhanced by your book. Every paragraph, and even each sentence, makes me stop and think, reflect on my understanding of life and the indivisible whole. Reading *Sensation of Oneness* is like re-reading the thousands of books I read in my life with new light. *Thank you for the opportunity to reflect so deeply. I needed it.*"

—**Taku Nishimae,** Co-Founder, 1Future

"As a co-founder with me of Calvert Social Investment Fund, Terry has long keyed on the issues of compassion and of our interconnectedness though finances and otherwise. In this book, he definitely leads us into our potential next layer of maturity of both!"

—**Wayne Silby,** Founding Chair, Calvert Funds (Ret.)

"Terry Mollner's *Sensation of Oneness* is a practical guide to self-mastery of the skill of human self-consciousness. It is a prerequisite to fully grasp the universe operates as an individual whole. Once known, it holds the key to solving many of today's challenges, not the least of which is the underlying crisis of the maturation of all of humanity in this skill, the skill of human self-consciousness itself."

—**Paul Polman,** CEO 2009-2019, Unilever; Author,
*Net Positive: How Courageous Companies Thrive by Giving
More Than They Take*

"This book is an invitation to life-changing and world-changing ways of thinking. An invitation to trade our invented assumption that the universe operates as separate parts for the truth the universe in fact operates as an indivisible whole. The ten questions in this book of few words showed me how to "self-elder" myself into *full maturity* in the skill of human self-consciousness. Wonderful!"

—**Meesha Brown**
PCI Media, President

"This is an ambitious endeavor of love. Terry has sought to gift the reader, through the simple act of absorbing this work, a glimpse of the interrelatedness, interconnectedness, and interdependence of and between things. At the same time, he makes us aware that this is a critical step in the evolution of aware and responsible action, and therefore an imperative in achieving personal and collective peace."

—**Ketan Patel,** Founder and Chairman, Force for Good;
CEO, Greater Pacific Capital

"We live in an era of climate crises, polarised societies, and failed leadership. What is required is completely new perspectives from which we can mature the fabric of our existence as human beings. In *"Sensation of Oneness,"* Terry Mollner, a pioneering businessman with vast experience in working for the common good on the global scene, teaches us with great pedagogy and care how to learn "the skill of human self-consciousness." His insights enable us to relate with the way the universe operates. This is an important contribution to new perspectives needed to both mature our personal journey and enhance our collective social progress."

—**Björn Larsson,** CEO, The ForeSight Group,
Co-author of *Changing the World We Create, The Rise of the Meaningful Economy*

"In this book pioneer responsible investor and asset manager, Terry Mollner, leads us toward the likely future of capitalism. We agree that cooperation is the framework for all human activities and especially in the evolution of markets and corporations. Based on his deep experience, Mollner describes how corporations, while fully doing both, will progress toward giving priority to the common good and second priority to competition."

—**Hazel Henderson,** President, Ethical Markets Media (USA & Brazil)
Author of *Mapping the Global Transition to the Solar Age*

"Only through the maturation of each of us in our skill of human self-consciousness can we successfully tackle the profound challenges confronting humanity and our planet. Terry Mollner's wonderful new book is an outstanding guide to this journey. Make sure you do not miss out on this valuable map to fulfilling both your potential and the joy of participating the planet's potential."

—**Jeffery Hollender,** Co-founder and former CEO, Seventh Generation
Co-founder and CEO, American Sustainable Business Council

"Behind a world full of harm is human beings who are living a collective crisis of consciousness. Terry Mollner, an elder in the social business community, devotes his energy in this book to sharing his views of what can lead to "self-conscious "eldering", a process that he sees as able to expand our collective consciousness."

—**Morgan Simon,** Impact Investor
Author of *Real Impact: The New Economics of Social Change*

Copyright © 2021 by Trust Funds for All Children, Inc.

Published and distributed in the United States by THE LOVE SKILL Publishing,
PO Box 631 Shutesbury, MA 01072
www.sensationofoneness.org

All right reserved. No part of this book may be used or reproduced by any mechanical, photographic or electronic process, or in the form of an audio recording; nor may it be stored in a retrieval system, transmitted or otherwise be copied for public use, other than for fair use as brief quotations embodied in articles and reviews without prior written permission of the author.

Cover design: Greg Caulton
Interior layout: Frances Lassor

Printed by Kindle Direct Publishing

Sensation of Oneness / Terry Mollner

ISBN-13: 9798760651341

Printed in the United States of America

$19.95 US

To all those who are self-eldering themselves
to full maturity in the
skill of human self-consciousness.

A Personal Note

Today, before reading a book, many people like to know the person who is writing it. I will write some paragraphs here to introduce myself to you. (One publisher rejected this book with the words, "It is a good book, but you are not famous enough.") I am not famous. However, I think you will like knowing the following about me before reading this book. Of course, if you are not at this time interested in learning about me and how I came to write this book, jump to the *Preface*. It describes the three new and not widely known facts upon which this book is based.

I am now 77 years old. Like your life I suspect, my life has been divided into my public front office and my private back office. My front office is my roles in organizations and accomplishments. They are listed in a description of me in the materials of organizations where I am fulfilling or have fulfilled a role. What I have been doing in my private back office is what you will learn about me when reading this book. Its activities culminated in my discovery I could know, and as a skill choose to give priority to, the sensation of the reality of the oneness of nature.

The latter is a fact that is now the most popular theory in fundamental physics (the Holographic Theory). By default, it is a result of their discovery time and space (the assumption of separate parts) are mutually agreed upon illusion tools we invented. However, what it is pointing at is not primarily a theory or, for some, a spiritual belief. It is primarily pointing at a sensation we can be aware of and consistently know as the sensation within which we experience all other experiences.

In the next four paragraphs I will summarize what I have learned, and you could learn when reading this book. You may experience it as heady. Prepare yourself. It is heady. It will only be four paragraphs, but at this time it is the most concise presentation in words I am able to provide of what I have learned.

Enjoying the sensation of oneness is the skill of each moment *primarily experiencing* the three-dimensionality of the oneness of nature instead of the two-dimensionality of words. Frankly, it is that simple. However, until you have mastered in the natural sequence the smaller skills of each of the layers of maturity of the skill of human self-consciousness, and integrate them into the one fully mature skill, you can't easily choose this as a skill you can consistently use and enjoy. (Herein I define "human self-consciousness" as knowing what we are doing while we are doing it and able to exercise free choice, eventually individual free choice, and later what will be described as mature free choice.)

I can now be consistently aware of and enjoy the sensation of oneness. It is the experience within which I experience the fundamental feelings that are a result of being able to give it priority: natural confidence, contented joy, and compassion. They are now more important than relative feelings of some derivatives of mad, glad, sad, and scared. By skill and choice, experiencing relative feelings are now third in priority, and using words is now fourth in priority. As you can see, this is the opposite of giving priority to the two-dimensionality of words.

Between learning words in childhood and achieving full maturity in this skill, I was giving priority to the mutually agreed upon illusions of words. There are over 6,000 human languages on Earth. Each is a set of mutually agreed upon illusion tools, labeled "words," that allow those using them to be self-conscious parts of the indivisible universe. Maturing in the skill of human self-consciousness is a result of learning and using words. Using them was necessary for me to master the remaining smaller skills of the layers of maturity of it in the natural sequence to achieve full maturity in it. (But I am only good at it on Tuesdays and Thursdays!) While fully and simultaneously doing both of the following, it resulted in me giving priority to the self-consciousness of being the indivisible universe and second priority to the self-consciousness of being my physical body part of it. As you will discover, the first is the result of exercising mature free choice and the second is the result of exercising individual free choice.

The purpose of this book is to use words and guided experiences to assist you to master full maturity in this skill, the skill of human self-consciousness.

Those were the four paragraphs. At this time that is my best short summary of what I have learned in my private back office. It is also what you could learn from reading this book and doing the experiential activities in it.

(I searched hard my entire life to find a person who could help me in my self-eldering process to achieve full maturity in this skill. I never found someone who could do it. By default, I had to discover it on my own in the school of hard knocks. I am writing this book so future children can be skillfully and artfully eldered by their parents and others into full maturity in this most important skill for them to learn before they leave home. We now know their brains are sufficiently developed by their twenties to accomplish it.)

I can summarize my main roles and accomplishments in my front office in only five paragraphs. Then I will tell some of the stories of how I consistently backed into discovering some of the smaller skills of each next layer of maturity of the higher layers of this skill.

Here are those five paragraphs.

I am a co-founder of what is now a company with $37 billion under management and of a foundation that has loaned nearly $3 billion to reduce poverty. I am also the person who took the lead to save Ben & Jerry's to live on as a boldly socially responsible company once it had to live inside a multinational corporation. Because of expansion into other countries, to solve its growing distribution problems it had to get bought by one of them: this became a problem for all our socially responsible companies once they became that successful.

Those are always listed as my main accomplishments, and the interesting part is I didn't set out to do all three of them with any thought of making money. Here, in each case, is what I was primarily thinking about.

In the 1970s, I thought we needed to have an option in the investment community of investing in companies that are making the world a better place instead of a worse place. That became the Calvert Family of Socially Responsible Mutual Funds, now known only as the Calvert Funds. In the 1980s, I thought we needed a foundation that borrowed money at low interest rates and consistently loaned it, not granted it, at low interest rates to reduce poverty around the world. That was the Calvert foundation, now known as Calvert Impact Capital. In 2000, I thought Ben & Jerry's, the best-known flagship of our socially responsible business community of the last half of the 20th century, needed to survive once inside a multinational as a boldly socially responsible company.

The Calvert Funds was the first family of socially responsible mutual funds on Earth. Thankfully, that movement has now gone mainstream. Calvert Impact Capital was the first charitable non-profit to raise money at low interest rates to be consistently re-loaned at low interest rates to reduce poverty by raising the money through the national community of brokers, asset managers, and both small and large investors. Ben & Jerry's, even to this day, is the only socially responsible company bought by a multinational to sign a legal contract that guaranteed it could continue forever as an independent and boldly socially responsible company. It can even take social positions on issues with which Unilever, who bought us, disagrees.

The important thing for you to take note of about my participation in these three firsts is, if I had gone to a business school, I probably wouldn't have thought I could accomplish any of them: all three had never been done before. The second thing you should take note of is I accomplished being part of starting the first two when I was still in my late twenties and early 30s and usually living on about $5,000 a year. I was living frugally in group houses, didn't have an automobile, and never experienced my basic needs not being met. (I am fond of saying to people who ask me when I am going to retire, "I can't retire because I haven't begun to work!")

There are others, but these are my main roles and accomplishments listed in a description of me in the back of the materials of these organizations.

Now for the most important part of who I am. In my back office my priority was what as a sophomore in high school I described as "discovering the meaning of life."

Here is the story of how that happened.

I was one of the first boys from the working class and ethnic communities in South Omaha, Nebraska, USA, to be accepted into the all-boys Catholic Jesuit high school, Creighton Prep. It was in the wealthy part of town. I had also accomplished the most prestigious thing of being on the football team that at that time usually won the state championship.

One day two guys on the football team I greatly respected, Jim and Larry, and I were given permission during lunch period to go to our lockers to get our history books to study for a test. When Jim said he had learned milk causes pimples, with great enthusiasm I exclaimed "Really!!!" In hindsight, I now realize I was fully giving my power to choose away. I was behaving as the lower-class person I thought I was in relationship to them. They fell all over the hallway hysterically laughing at my gullibility and lower-class behavior. I felt like a puddle anyone could walk through.

When open, my locker door blocked my view of them at their lockers. When I got my history book and closed my locker door, all I saw was their backsides as they ran through the swinging doors that led back to the cafeteria. Seeking an escape from everything, I ducked into the nearby chapel to avoid going back to the cafeteria.

While sitting in the last pew and tears falling on my pants, I eventually asked myself this question, "Who can I say loves me?" I couldn't think of anyone who behaved lovingly toward me.

It was an overcast day, but in the darkness of the chapel I could see the crucifix over the alter and realized there was one person who loved me. God loved me! I got up on the kneeler and smiled in appreciation there was one person I could say loved me. Then just as quickly I slid back into sitting on the pew and realized that hadn't made any difference when those two fellow football players were cruel to me.

After a period of thinking, I got back up on the kneeler and admitted to myself I was ignorant. I didn't know why to do one thing rather than another. I decided I was going to take the first vow in my life. (A vow was what I understood to be the deepest level of agreement with myself.)

I would give priority to "discovering the meaning of life," why to do one thing rather than another.

I then decided the strategy I would use to accomplish this goal. Each day I would attend Mass during the first part of lunch period to think for the purpose of figuring out the meaning of life. I did that the rest of my high school years and all during my years at Creighton University.

In my more important back office, up to now discovering the meaning of life has remained my priority my entire life. As you will soon read, now it is Eldering.

As you can imagine, the Jesuits loved witnessing me going to Mass every day and I eventually left Creighton University to enter the Jesuit seminary to study to be a Catholic priest. When I agreed to do it, I was clear with Father Haley my priority was to discover the meaning of life. He assured me I would be free to give that priority. Not only that. He also said they would strongly support me in that quest, including getting a doctorate in any field I wanted.

In the seminary, they wouldn't let me read some of the books I wanted to read, especially one by a fellow Jesuit, Pierre Teilhard de Chardin, who had been inspired by Eastern spirituality. I then realized they were training me to be a salesperson of their beliefs. I also concluded they had not only broken their agreement with me but because of this agenda were incapable of keeping it. I left.

When I returned to Creighton University and settled back into being there, I wanted to take some time to fully understand what had happened that had me end up in the Jesuit seminary. To think things through, one night I took a long walk on the circular path the Jesuits use for walking meditation in the garden behind the administration building.

I realized I had made the mistake of giving my power to choose to the Catholic Church. I thought the Jesuits were the one group I could trust to keep an agreement. I now knew they hadn't been dishonest. Instead, because of their beliefs they were incapable of keeping it. I also realized, like the Jesuits, nearly every person I knew was trying to sell me something. I became clear I did not want to again make the mistake of giving my power to choose to another person or group.

(Again, in hindsight, I can see this was a reaction to the pain of the Jesuits breaking their agreement with me. However, my decision was a good one: I would no longer trust any individual or group with my power to choose. Instead, I would keep it and only study my direct experiences to identify the facts I would use to guide my thinking.)

This meant I had to throw out all my self-consciously chosen and, as much as possible, unconscious beliefs in my thinking and start from scratch. I was now fully willing to do that.

I also concluded there were two truths I already knew. First, I will only study my direct experiences to identify the facts I will use to guide my thinking. Secondly, I judged it was obvious there was always a reason to do one thing rather than another. With these first two beliefs I would start from scratch to build a set of beliefs to guide my thinking. This became the second vow I took with myself.

(Again, in hindsight, I think this was unconsciously a result of having learned facts were best found using science. It was determining them from a repeated study of present experiences. However, I was not using professional science, facts discovered by others. I was unconsciously using what I would label being a "personal scientist" by using "mature free choice." It is the exercise of free choice that assumes oneness is a fact. Both will be described in the *Preface*. I now realize at twenty-one years old I had backed into giving priority to being a personal scientist and didn't know it.)

As I was leaving the garden, it suddenly hit me that, if I was throwing out all my current beliefs, I had to also throw out my belief there is a God. That had me stop and return to the garden and again walk around its circular path. It eventually became clear to me I could not solely give priority to finding the facts to guide my life in direct experiences if I kept any belief I couldn't repeatedly confirm was a fact in direct experiences. I also concluded if God exists, I will eventually experience God in direct experiences.

Dropping my belief there is a God was experienced as a big decision. But I realized this: if I was going to now give priority to only using facts to guide my thinking I could repeatedly confirm are facts in my direct experiences, I had to also throw out my belief there is a God.

I eventually left the garden comfortable in keeping my second vow to only give priority to discovering in direct experiences additional facts I would use to guide my thinking. (I did eventually discover in my direct experiences what I label "God," but now God is not anything like what I believed God was then. I also learned to be comfortable not knowing what I don't know. There is much you do not need to know and are still able to achieve full maturity in the skill of human self-consciousness, such as a direct experience of what you label "God.")

When I returned to Creighton University, I also got frustrated at how slow learning occurred in classes. I began to go to the library, find the shelves of the books about something I wanted to learn, put twenty to thirty books on a borrowed library cart, spend an hour or so going through all of them to understand the full territory, and then left the library with two or three books I thought could provide me what I wanted to learn. In other words, I began to boldly take charge of my self-education.

I later learned I was better at thinking the most important things through on my own rather than primarily getting the answers to these questions from books written by others. For instance, when I was about thirty years old and new to the world of finance, I thought I should learn more about money in our lives. I took a day off to walk back and forth in my large bedroom at the time, talking out loud to not lose my train of thought and fill in any gaps, and think myself into understanding the basics about money. I had never thought much about money, and I didn't like most of my fellow university students in business school because I thought they thought about it too much. (And they wore those heavy wingtip shoes! I may have been the first hippie in Omaha, Nebraska! But I also wasn't aware of those values emerging inside me at that time.)

I concluded there was not a good reason why doctors, lawyers, and business executives made much more than waitresses and garbage collectors. It was just what had happened and didn't have to be that way. I secondly discovered the most valuable thing I would have if I had a lot of money: free time to do whatever I wanted to do. Thirdly, I realized by living frugally I had already accomplished that!

It was during this day-long walk back and forth in my bedroom, where out my window I could see some of the downtown Boston skyline of tall buildings and a little bit of the Atlantic Ocean, that I concluded I should continue to give priority to following my heart to discover the meaning of life. I had already accomplished what much money would give me! I was not only free to do whatever I wanted to do but also free to give priority to what I most enjoyed doing. I was intuitively giving priority to doing anything I thought would both allow me to mature and make the world a better place for all rather than doing things where the priority was to make money.

It also became clear to me not only should I never give priority to making money, but I should also not be concerned about how much comes through me. What is most important is it never be my priority. It is a unit of measurement for exchanges with which I could buy anything. It is not giving priority to living a beautiful mature human life.

(Again, in hindsight, I was also not aware I was doing something very important you will read about when you read this book. I was giving priority to priorities, the pattern of thinking of oneness, instead of the pattern of thinking of the assumption of separate parts, this-or-that-in-times-and-places. Somehow, I had backed into also doing this.)

As you can easily imagine, to some degree this also explains why I didn't get married until I was 49 years old. My priority was following my heart and every woman I was with eventually looked at me with that look of, "You don't get it! Life is about a house in the suburbs, 2.5 children, a two-car garage, and a white picket fence?" Well, that is what it felt like to me—a business deal—each time she or I had to end a romantic relationship or when I had to end my first marriage. I was clear I was not going to commit to being with someone who was not also giving priority to discovering the meaning of life and comfortable living frugally if necessary to keep it our priority.

(I was with my first wife for twenty years from when I was thirty-seven years old, getting married only when 49 years old, and we still have a very close friendship. I co-raised her daughter, Jaime, from the age of seven years old. Her birth father and I are good friends, and I play a second grandfather role for her two children, Gram (age 9) and Lila Pearl (age 7). I also play a full father role for Stella (age 16). She is the daughter of a Lesbian couple who asked me to be a fully active father of the baby they wanted me to help them birth. In case you want to know how we did it, they provided me a ball jar and, with the equivalent of a turkey baster, they did it themselves. I know, TMI. But I thought you might like to know how we did it. You now know me as "Mr. Frugal": this didn't cost us a penny!)

Having lived in group houses with many divorced people who often saw their children only on weekends and were unable to do strong co-parenting with their former spouse, I was not willing to be in a committed relationship where we did not know the skill of consistently experiencing the joy of love and able to together do wise parenting. With each lover we were never able to figure out how to discover and invite ourselves into knowing that experience with each other as a skill we could sustain. By the time I was 70 years old, I had given up and concluded I would remain single the rest of my life. I judged I had more important things to do than continually taking the time to be exploring the possibility of a committed romantic relationship. As you will see below, that changed when I met Lucy.

I could tell many more stories from my life adventures but, before I tell you the story of meeting Lucy, let me point out a few other things I learned along the way you might like to know about me before reading this book.

First, I learned early on I could learn much more by being with people who were not like me than being with people who were like me. Therefore, I was always up for adventures to go to different places and joining different organizations with different people. Secondly, and also for that purpose, I valued traveling around the world to experience people living in very different ways than we do in the USA. I discovered much from being in other cultures. Thirdly, I have often begun experiments to learn things. The most important ones were being part of beginning three intentional communities. My goal was to discover how to re-village our lives in our modern context. I also went from being a high school teacher of theater and directing musicals, to being an actor, singer, and model in Chicago (I was in a four-page foldout in *Playboy*, it was a natural gas ad!), to substantial training to be a psychotherapist, to being a social and financial activist.

Since 2000, and after witnessing first-hand for months the sophisticated dishonesty on Wall Street when doing the Ben & Jerry's negotiations, I realized I was one of the few people who had been deeply involved in spirituality, psychotherapy, community building, business, and finance. Therefore, I also judged I may be one of the people who could figure out how to take our human lives and organizations to the next layer of maturity possible for us. Because of these skills and experiences, and now having ample money, I concluded it was my moral responsibility to give priority to what I could do to have us accomplish this.

By that time, I also knew, fundamentally, this could only naturally, effortlessly, freely, and consistently occur in each human being by me discovering the higher layers of maturity of the skill of human self-consciousness and being able to introduce them to others. And in hindsight I realized discovering them had been my priority my entire life! I was all in. Accomplishing this became the third vow I made with myself.

I quit the boards I was on except the three main ones mentioned above, and my activities in other organizations, to focus on figuring out what the next layers of maturity for humanity might be. Since then, my discipline to remain focused on this has been writing books. They keep me thinking things through linearly, like when I was walking back and forth and talking out loud in my bedroom. I have written eight books, six of which have been self-published (I am not famous enough!) and the other two will eventually be self-published. That also allows me to provide them free on our website so people with cell phones all over the world can read them. This, however, is the book I was hoping I would be able to eventually write. It is also available on our website, www.sensationofoneness.org. (If you have bought one, thank you. You are funding this educational program.)

This is a short book that takes you, the reader, into learning the skills of mastering the last two layers of maturity of the skill of human self-consciousness. You probably already know the first five of the seven layers. Most people on Earth do. It also takes you into thinking about the ways it will change our romantic relationships, parenting, democracy, business, and ending poverty.

Finally, I thought I had figured it all out until I met Lucy. (I now know we are always ignorant of the next layer of maturity until we discover it in direct experiences, not only in words. In the meantime, we, self-consciously or unconsciously, think the layer we are operating on is the highest layer. This is especially true if we are not aware there are higher layers of maturity of this skill and, in relationship with the other layers, can identify the one we are currently operating on.) As mentioned above, I had given up on finding a woman with whom we could together figure out how to enjoy the experience of love.

Lucy and I had one of those love at first sight experiences. (Again, in hindsight, I now think the universe knows better what is best for me than I do. This has me now pay keen attention to its always occurring direct downloads of information into my thinking in sensations, feelings, and words. This reaction to meeting Lucy was one of the ways it kicked me in the butt to do what I needed to do to mature further. My assessment is most people on Earth today are not aware self-consciousness is a skill, there are layers of maturity of smaller skills to master it, and they are aware of the highest layers of maturity of it. I had fooled myself into thinking I had mastered the highest layer and, as you will see, I didn't know I was still giving priority to words. Therefore, I was still operating at the sixth of the seven layers of it and didn't know it.)

Lucy and I agreed we would not explore the traditional way of doing a romantic relationship. Instead, we agreed to consistently give priority in our relationship to what we both experienced as "the joy of love at first sight" and see what it could teach us.

I was fully aware the joy we experienced of love at first sight was the exact joy I wanted us to always know! It was the exact joy I wanted us to learn to know as a skill we could always choose as the container experience of our relationship! That was it! I had finally witnessed it naturally and effortlessly happening with someone! And I was now capable of always giving that joy priority in my relationship with Lucy to see what it could teach us! As you can witness as I tell the story here, I was very excited Lucy was willing to join me in this experiment. She did not understand it as I did. Today she says she was just "smitten" with me. However, she was fully aware of us having had the experience of "the joy of love at first sight" and willing to trust in me and it.

By this time, I understood the importance of giving priority to priorities in my thinking, and that was why I was able to consistently give that recognized joy priority in our relationship. As you will discover, it is the pattern of thinking of the assumption of oneness. As described earlier and now a skill, I had learned how to give it priority over the pattern of thinking of assuming separate parts. This is one of the main smaller skills we learn at the sixth layer of maturity of the skill of human self-consciousness. Therefore, I knew how to consistently do it.

It took me more than three years of giving priority to this joy to learn what it could teach us. I was seeking to discover what it was as a *skill* I could learn and consistently choose to execute.

I made several wrong guesses. Each time I had to again return to giving priority to the joy of love at first sight to sustain the experience of love in our relationship. Eventually I discovered what you will read as the four smaller skills of the Mature Elder layer of maturity. It is the last and highest layer I still had not discovered but thought I had! (I did not know I was still unconsciously, without choice, giving priority to words. I did not know sensation is the most self-consciously able to be experienced *direct relationship* with the rest of the universe.)

Then, one morning while meditating in the hot tub on our deck as I do each morning around 4am, I suddenly popped into experiencing the sauna shed in the yard as a three-dimensional sensation. I instantly realized that was a different experience than the way I just moments earlier was experiencing it. I then realized I had been previously experiencing it as a two-dimensional experience, as existing as a separate part in times and places. I had been unaware I had been *primarily seeing the words "sauna shed"* when looking at it and not *primarily experiencing it in the realm of sensation*, my most direct relationship with the other parts of the universe.

I then realized giving priority to experiencing it as a *three-dimensional sensation* was including the third dimension of oneness. I was now experiencing the sauna shed in times, places, and oneness and giving priority to the third one, the sensation of oneness. I realized I had popped into automatically doing that because, having already mastered the smaller skills at the sixth layer, I knew oneness is real and the assumption of separate parts is a mutually agreed upon illusion tool we invented. Thus, when including oneness, I naturally gave second priority to experiencing it as a separate part. While fully experiencing all three dimensions of times, places, and oneness being present, the total experience was primarily *a self-consciously known sensation, not primarily words.* (In hindsight, I now know this discovery could not have happened if I had not already mastered the smaller skills at the sixth layer. The smaller skills of each layer can only build on the mastery of the smaller skills of the previous layer.)

Finally, I realized that up to that moment in my life I had been unconsciously (without choice) always giving priority to words rather than reality, *the three-dimensional sensation of self-consciously known oneness.* I also realized I could experience it as the container within which the illusion of separate parts exist that allows me to be self-conscious.

Later, when Lucy woke up and came down to the kitchen, I gave priority to experiencing her and our relationship as a three-dimensional sensation. *Without effort, we were instantly in that joy of love at first sight experience.* I then more strongly realized it was not primarily words. It was primarily a sensation. I realized I had discovered what giving that joy priority for more than three years had taught me: *reality is including oneness in all I see and do, and I can execute is as a skill by experiencing everything as primarily a three-dimensional sensation.* That is adding the reality of oneness into a cooperative combination with the assumption of separate parts and words. That combination allows me to know the reality of oneness as a *self-consciously known sensation.* Not primarily a belief in words or feeling, but primarily a sensation, my physical body's most direct relationship with the rest of the universe.

Not only that. Having discovered it using mature free choice, solely from a repeated study of my present experiences, I could now confidently know it, name it, choose it, learn to do it as a skill, and have it become a habit. Wow! I wanted to do the happy dance throughout the house!

With Lucy all morning long I kept noticing I no longer needed to give priority to our joy of love at first sight to experience it. It was now effortlessly present, and I was able to have it be present both as a *choice* and as a *skill* I could execute.

I looked around the room. Everywhere I looked I experienced everything occurring in the now self-consciously known three-dimensional sensation of oneness. I later realized I had discovered full maturity in the skill of human self-consciousness is primarily experiencing everything occurring in the sensation of three-dimensionality. But I did not know that then. I would only later learn more of what I needed to know to have the necessary fundamental opposites fully present and not in conflict with each other: two-dimensionality (the assumption of separate parts) and three-dimensionality (the assumption of oneness). You will learn how to do that when you read this book. I had discovered it, but I did not yet have full maturity in it as a skill. There was more I needed to know to master it as a skill and turn it into a habit.

Ever since I have nearly always (of course there are times when I lose it) known and experienced the joy of the sensation of oneness as the container of all Lucy and I do in our relationship. We now know the sensation of oneness is not between the two of us. There is only one oneness. It is everywhere and we now know how to live self-consciously inside it together.

Lucy is not as introspective and intellectually oriented as I am, but she loves enjoying the joyful sensation of oneness with me! And we love enjoying it together! And that is what matters. Everything else is of such secondary importance, I notice I don't ever give any of it serious attention. Each moment I give priority to fully accepting Lucy as she is and fully enjoy the skill of having the joy of love be the container of all we do together. (I have been in a men's group for twenty-six years. Going against their encouragement to do it, the last seven years I have told them I wouldn't do Match.com, but I would happily respond to love if it happened with someone. I am glad I stayed true to that agreement with myself.)

Lastly, I discovered something else also. It takes another self-consciously skilled person to know it with me to confirm for both it is real and not a fantasy of desire. When I primarily experience my relationship with Lucy as a self-consciously known three-dimensional sensation, and she responds affirming it as real and beautiful by joyfully joining me there, I know it is real and not a fantasy of desire. Experiencing it with the sauna shed was not enough. I needed it confirmed as mutually experienced as real with another self-consciously skilled human being as something we could *mutually know and choose within the realm of self-consciousness.* This is probably why people find attractive the joy of the mutual love experience with another person and the raising of children. It is a confirmation they are mutually living in the more mature realm of self-consciousness rather than just being conscious. The latter is doing what they naturally do at the highest layer of maturity of this skill they know. At the same time, lacking full maturity in the skill of human self-consciousness is why so many fail to sustain that joy as the container of all they do together.

Lucy and I now enjoy the sensation of oneness all day each day. I also know if I had used a checklist in my thinking to choose Lucy, our romantic relationship would never have happened. I only discovered what a perfect match we are after living together for years. I now know maturation cannot be escaped or stopped. Doing this experiment with Lucy is how that natural process of maturation showed me the way to master the last layer smaller skills I still hadn't discovered. (I was very humbled by this. I was sure I had already discovered it, unaware I had only discovered it in words.)

I want you and your lover to know the skill of full maturity in the skill of human self-consciousness. Then the two of you have the option of mutually choosing to consistently experience the joy of love as the sensation of oneness within which you experience all other experiences. It will also reveal how to come back to it when one of you, or both of you, lose giving it priority. It is the skill of knowing how to give priority, individually and mutually, to the sensation of oneness that is always everywhere and able to be experienced. It is not something between the two of you. I now know it can only happen as a skillful self-conscious choice upon mastering the full skill of human self-consciousness. It is possible the two of you could learn these skills from reading this book and trying on the experiences I will guide you into experiencing.

Each moment and wherever you are, I also want you to have the joy of participating in the maturation of our human species on Earth. That joy also can only be consistently achieved by mastering the highest layer of maturity of the skill of human self-consciousness. Then you will not be able to stop yourself from giving priority in your thinking and actions to what throughout history has most often been labeled "Eldering." It will also be described in the *Preface*. I think you will discover each moment there is nothing more enjoyable than Eldering.

Today, this is how I see who I am. I hope you choose to read this book and use it as one of your tools to achieve full maturity in the skill of human self-consciousness. We now know how each of us can self-elder ourselves into mastering the last two layers of it that up to now have not been widely known and mastered. As I think you will also eventually agree, they will soon be widely known and mastered by many.

I think you will also eventually agree maturation cannot be escaped or stopped. It is the fundamental process in this rascally indivisible universe.

Preface

Please Read This
Before Reading This Book

When you repeatedly answer the 10 questions in the first few one-page chapters of this book, you discover it is obvious the universe operates as an indivisible whole. You also discover this is the exact opposite assumption you were operating on during most of your childhood. And you may still be operating on it. To learn words during those first years it was necessary to operate on the opposite assumption. It is that the universe is separate parts.

The discovery of this fact necessitates you train yourself, what will be labeled "self-eldering," into operating on this accurate and opposite assumption. This is a full reversal of the fundamental assumption you used in your thinking to learn words. That was wonderful! They allowed you to be a self-conscious part of the indivisible universe.

Everything is conscious. Each is doing what it naturally does and keeps doing it. Only human beings have invented human words that allow us to be what we can label "self-conscious." It is knowing what our physical bodies are doing while they are doing it and able to exercise free choice. Later it is maturing into exercising individual free choice and eventually what will be labeled "mature free choice." The latter will be described below.

It is not possible to master what I have identified as the last two of the seven layers of maturity of the skill of human self-consciousness until the fact the universe operates as an indivisible whole is discovered in a study of one's direct experiences. Therefore, repeatedly answering the 10 questions is important. They reveal it is *obvious* the universe operates as an indivisible whole. If it wasn't, we could not have been naturally and effortlessly breathing since we came out of our mothers' wombs.

The primary purpose of this book is to assist you in your self-eldering process to achieve full maturity in the skill of human self-consciousness.

No one else can do it for you. Since your mastery of what will be labeled the Teen layer of maturity, your physical body has the skill of exercising individual free choice. Thus, since the layers of maturity build on one another, only your physical body can self-elder itself into full maturity in this skill by exercising its ability and right of individual free choice.

It begins with answering the 10 questions to discover it is obvious the universe operates as an indivisible whole. You can then, and only then, self-elder yourself into the mastery of the smaller skills of the last two layers. They necessitate operating on that assumption. With mature parenting by your parents and others, your physical body can achieve full maturity in this skill by the end of your teenage years. If you are older, self-eldering yourself into full maturity in this skill will not take a long time. The amount of time is determined by the amount of time you make it a priority of your self-conscious attention. The latter is the greatest power of your physical body.

This book is based on three facts I will describe below that are now not widely known. However, they will soon be widely known. Using words, what we label "facts" are the only things we can all eventually agree are facts. For instance, we all agree rocks are hard, fire is hot, and the Earth is round. And I believe we will soon use words to all also agree the below three facts are facts.

As I trust you will also eventually agree, cooperation of the parts of the indivisible universe for its maturation, not competition among the illusion of separate parts, is the fundamental process in nature. And maturation cannot be escaped or stopped. Therefore, just as nearly all human beings have been eldered into the mastery of what will be labeled the Baby, Toddler, Child, Teen, and Adult layer skills of human self-consciousness, at some point in the future nearly all will be eldered into full maturity in this skill. Just about anywhere you look—at marriage, parenting, democracy, economics, technology, and ending poverty—when thinking of Earth as a whole maturation has not been able to be escaped or stopped.

The first not widely known fact is we now know the universe operates as an indivisible whole.

Fortunately, through a convoluted process the now most popular fact in fundamental physics is time and space (the assumption the universe is separate parts) are mutually agreed upon illusion tools we invented. By default, the assumption is the universe operates as an indivisible whole. This is called the "Holographic Theory." This will now not only be seen as the most fundamental spiritual and religious belief of many but also as the most fundamental fact in physics. By answering the 10 questions, you will also discover this fact can at any time be observed to be a fact in your present experience.

The second not widely known fact is operating on the assumption the universe is separate parts was a result of our invention of words.

They, you will discover, were a by-product of our discovery of *the greater joy of experiencing mutual self-consciousness.* It is then words that allow us to mature into the last two layers of maturity of this skill. That is where we *freely choose* to operate on the now self-consciously known fact represented in one of many ways in words as "the universe operates as an indivisible whole."

We then discover the assumption of separate parts we have been unconsciously (without choice) operating on up to this point was *a mutually agreed upon illusion tool we were unaware we had also invented when we invented words.* For instance, the word "tree" must be both *different and separate* from the word "rock" and the word "river." We now also know this was the most valuable tool we invented! It has allowed us to be the parts of the indivisible universe with the skill of human self-consciousness. As stated above, this is the skill of knowing what we are doing while we are doing it and able to exercise free choice, later individual free choice, and eventually mature free choice that will be described below.

There are only two ways to represent in human language the way the universe could be structured: as separate parts or as an indivisible whole. Think it through for yourself: there is not a third option. It is necessary to operate on the assumption it is separate parts to master the skill of inventing and using human words. They, in turn, allow us to achieve full maturity in the skill of human self-consciousness.

It is to freely choose to operate on the now self-consciously known fact the universe operates as an indivisible whole.

During the first five layers of maturation in this skill, the Baby, Toddler, Child, Teen, and Adult layers, we are still operating on the assumption the universe is separate parts.

From scientific research we now also know only in our teenage years are our physical bodies sufficiently developed to where we can discover and master the last two layers of the seven layers of maturity of it. Herein they are named the Elder and Mature Elder layers. They are based on the discovery of the *fact* the universe operates as an indivisible whole and, therefore, the assumption it is separate parts is a mutually agreed upon illusion tool we invented. It allowed us to invent and use words that, in turn, allowed us to mature in the skill of human self-consciousness to where we can discover, *and now freely and self-consciously choose to operate on,* the fact the universe operates as an indivisible whole. We now also realize this is the opposite assumption from what we were assuming that allowed us to master the first five layers.

At the beginning of this book, I will guide you into using mature free choice to answer 10 questions that will have you discover the fact it is obvious the universe operates as an indivisible whole. You may discover you are still unconsciously (without choice) operating on the assumption necessary to master the first five layers of maturity of this skill. Up to now in history, nearly all of humanity has remained operating on that assumption, that is, operating at the Adult layer or lower. The purpose of this book is to serve as a handbook you can use to self-elder yourself into the mastery of the last two layers. As stated above, because they build on your ability and right to exercise individual free choice, to achieve full maturity in the skill of human self-consciousness no one can master those two layers for you.

The third fact is our skill of using words that allows us to mature in the skill of human self-consciousness is a skill.

It is not, as it has been thought, a biological mutation thousands of years ago. Like chimpanzees teach their young the right size rock to use to crack open nuts, we teach our children the smaller skills of each layer of maturity of the skill of human self-consciousness as far up the layers as we know. And it is not a simple skill like learning to use a spoon or chopsticks. It is a complex skill with many smaller skills that must be learned in the natural sequence and eventually integrated together into the one full skill.

For instance, when learning the complex skill of riding a bicycle, we can't learn to peddle a bike while remaining balanced on it until we have learned to remain balanced sitting on it as it rolls forward. In the same natural sequence, we can't learn to use what will be described below as "mature free choice" to discover the fact the universe operates as an indivisible whole until we have learned to exercise individual free choice.

To be affirming the above three facts, three-fourths of the way through the *Introduction* I will switch from me writing this book to the fact it is the indivisible universe that is *primarily* writing it. If the universe is an indivisible whole, it is the only thing that is real. Separate parts do not exist. Therefore, the universe is primarily doing everything. As stated above and will be described in the beginning of the *Introduction*, the assumption the universe is separate parts was *a tool we invented*. It allowed us to, first, mutually enjoy self-consciousness, secondly invent words to confirm we were agreeing with each other we were mutually enjoying it, and thirdly, and as a result, be capable of achieving full maturity in the skill of human self-consciousness.

I am beginning the process of learning to give priority to the fact the universe operates as an indivisible whole. I also think it is time for all of us to mature to have this assumption present in our daily conversations. Therefore, three-fourths of the way through the *Introduction* I will explain why I will from that point forward operate on the assumption it is the indivisible universe that is primarily writing this book because, *primarily*, it is doing everything. I invite you to go to our website and give me feedback if this was, or was not, helpful to your self-eldering process: www.sensationofoneness.org/feedback. This book, and some of my other books, can be read for free on our website. I want them to be available to all the people around the world who have access to a cell phone.

I will now describe mature free choice.

Mature free choice is keeping your power to choose within your physical body and repeatedly studying your present experiences to identify the most important facts you will use to guide your thinking. If the universe is an indivisible whole, there is not a second thing to receive your power to choose. Until oneness is discovered to be a fact, most people are still unconsciously giving it to their parents or a belief in words—a parent-substitute. When oneness is discovered to be a fact, your only option of choice that affirms this fact is primarily using mature free choice to identify the facts you will use to guide your thinking.

On the next page I describe the layers of maturity of the skill of human self-consciousness I have identified using mature free choice. However, you will discover your use of mature free choice will not allow you to give your power to choose to me or my descriptions of them.

To achieve full maturity in this skill, you must use mature free choice to repeatedly study your present experiences to discover what you think they are: there is not a second thing to receive your power to choose, including me and my words.

While equally valuing both of the following, you will discover this is maturing from giving priority to "professional science" to giving priority to what will be labeled "personal science." It is the result of your maturation into giving priority to mature free choice.

On the next page are what I, solely using mature free choice, have identified as the smaller skills of the layers of maturity of this skill. When you use mature free choice, you may agree they represent facts. You may also give them other names you prefer. That is not only fine but encouraged. It can be a way of affirming for yourself you have used mature free choice to discover they are facts. As stated above, and regardless of what names you choose, mastering this skill is mastering the smaller skills in the natural sequence that can result in them integrating together into the one fully mature skill of human self-consciousness.

That results in the discovery of the *sensation of oneness*. That, in turn, results in the discovery of the feelings you didn't know you could self-consciously experience, the *fundamental feelings* of natural confidence, contented joy, and compassion. They are then given priority over our *relative feelings*, those operating on the assumption of separate parts. They are derivatives of mad, glad, sad, and scared.

After achieving full maturity in this skill, for the rest of our lives the priority in our thinking and actions is what has been described throughout history as "Eldering." It is each moment giving priority to the action we each judge is our best choice of self-conscious participation in continuous cooperation with the other parts for the maturation of the indivisible universe. As mentioned above, I think you will also eventually agree cooperation for maturation of the indivisible whole, not competition for the self-interest of your physical body, is the fundamental process of the oneness of nature. Competition is not the opposite of cooperation but a lower form of cooperation for maturation. The latter is the fundamental process of the oneness of nature that can't be escaped or stopped.

I suggest you read **The Seven Layers of Human Maturation** chart from the bottom up, the sequence in which we learn them.

As stated earlier, my hope is this book becomes a handbook you use to self-elder yourself to full maturity in the skill of human self-consciousness. And concerning what I will later in this book describe as the now possible maturation of our romantic and parenting relationships, and our democratic and economic organizations, it is important to point out we can only mutually operate at the highest layer of human maturity we mutually know. It is this fact that has us, whenever we can, play an Eldering role in the lives of others. We also discover there is nothing more enjoyable than Eldering. It is self-consciously moving as one with all that exists.

The Seven Layers of Human Maturation

Maturation of the Universe Continues After Your Physical Body's Death

MATURE ELDER

Priority of your physical body is *enjoying the sensation of oneness. While fully doing both, it is the sensation of freely choosing to give priority to the three-dimensionality of oneness (reality) and second priority to the two-dimensionality of words (illusions.) This results in its priority in thinking and action being Eldering. It is each moment giving priority to its best action of self-conscious participation in cooperation with the other parts for the maturation of the indivisible universe, the fundamental process in nature. Sustaining the self-consciously experienced joy of the sensation of oneness by giving priority to Eldering is what has our physical body experience its human life as consistently meaningful. The sensation of being alive is now known as the sensation of oneness, the sensation of primarily being the indivisible universe, the only thing that is real.*

ELDER

Priority of your physical body is *using mature free choice to study its breathing to discover the accurate fundamental fact the universe operates as an indivisible whole and then getting all the words it uses, its self-definition, and primary pattern of thinking accurately representing this fact*

ADULT

Priority of your physical body is *our freely chosen accurate or inaccurate fundamental outside belief on how the universe operates*

TEEN

Priority of your physical body is *exercising individual free choice, inventing the options of choice, and participating in our shared responsibility of cooperation for the common good of society and nature*

CHILD

Priority of your physical body is ***getting what it wants*** *from learning a human language, thereby being self-conscious, and assuming its physical body is, like words, a separate part*

TODDLER

Priority of your physical body is ***reacting to differences,*** *eventually labeled derivatives of the basic relative feelings of mad, glad, sad, and scared*

BABY

Priority of your physical body is ***reacting to sensations***

Maturation of the Universe Was Happening Before Your Physical Body's Birth

Introduction

Before we had invented words, many thousands of years ago, imagine two of us human beings sitting in the shade of some palm trees. It was a delightfully warm afternoon, and our bellies were full. One of us was playing with a coconut and making the sound "wackowacko" several times. The other one of us thought she saw something interesting. She went over to him, put her hand on his hand on the coconut, and while looking him directly and steadily in the eyes she repeated the word "wackowacko" a few times. He continued looking her directly and steadily in the eyes and said "wackowacko" back to her a few times as well.

What is the only way we could have agreed on the invention of our first word "wackowacko" for a coconut?

I think the answer is instead of the experience of conflict we both experienced the eye-to-eye peacefulness of what today we call the "sensation of agreement," *the sensation of the two of us moving as one*. We were also agreeing on the first word, the word "wackowacko" for a coconut. It was the way we were *confirming for each other we were mutually aware* we were enjoying the pleasure of self-consciously agreeing to move as one. It was our first mutual enjoyment of what we can label *the experience of self-consciously chosen "local oneness."*

Our first thought is we were primarily inventing the word "wackowacko." But we had no use for it. We had no other words. Our *priority* when inventing it had to be something else.

*When we were inventing that word, it was the mutually self-consciously known sensation of local oneness that was a maturation beyond consciousness and into the greater pleasure of self-consciousness, **mutually knowing what we are doing while we are doing it**. In this case, it was experienced while inventing the word "wackowacko" for a coconut*

This is what we discovered was enjoyable about this process. Therefore, to continue having that more pleasurable experience of *mutual self-consciousness* we kept inventing more words.

When inventing words, the mutually enjoyable experience of self-consciousness was the result of the two of us knowing together what we were doing while we were doing it. This was more enjoyable than only being conscious, doing what we naturally do. Later, and after inventing many more words, self-consciousness and words allowed us to analyze the past, develop a plan for the future, and consistently execute it in the present, alone or with others. It also allowed us to choose the relationships between and among the words in our thinking. That is exercising free choice. It can lead to later enjoying the greater pleasure of individual free choice. And later still into the even greater pleasure of mature free choice, described in the *Preface* and will be more fully described below.

What was *enjoyable* about looking another in the eyes and agreeing on a word for something was not the invention of the word.

*It was the two of us self-consciously moving together as one, **a more mature experience of the fact of the oneness of nature**, that was a more pleasurable sensation and, therefore, the main reason we enjoyed doing it.*

Seeking to again experience it is what propelled us to seek to invent more words for things. *To mutually confirm we were mutually experiencing it, we had to be agreeing on something.* New words were the easiest thing on which to mutually experience agreement on something. Therefore, we continually sought the enjoyment of the more mature experience of self-consciousness, *a more mature experience of the reality of the oneness of nature,* by inventing more words.

At the time, what we were unaware we were also doing is operating on an assumption that is not accurate: the assumption the universe is separate parts described in the *Preface*. It is not possible to invent the word "tree" for a tree, "rock" for a rock, and "river" for a river without assuming the universe is separate parts. It is that assumption that allows us to invent a different sound and symbol for each of the parts of the universe. This is treating the parts as if they are separate from one another. Words, of course, are also separate from one another.

However, the universe is not separate parts. It is an indivisible whole.

In the first pages of this book, I will guide you into a process that will have you discover it is obvious it operates as an indivisible whole. Currently, most fundamental physicists agree it is the most fundamental fact in physics (the Holographic Theory). More on this later.

When we were inventing words, we were not aware we were also inventing the assumption the universe is separate parts. That is why, even to this day, many of us still operate as if we are each only our physical body. *Like words,* we are operating as if we are each a part separate from everything else. In doing so, we are giving our power to choose to *a belief in words* that we are *unconsciously* (without choice) assuming is another separate part because we are unconsciously assuming all parts are separate from one another until we learn they aren't. This leaves us with only one way to relate with it: obedience. *We no longer have our power to choose.* It now resides with our "fundamental belief in words" to which we have given it.

Of course, eventually we dislike not having our power to choose. It is this that has us search for and, hopefully, discover mature free choice.

Currently, I believe humanity is in the process of maturing from giving priority to individual free choice to giving priority to mature free choice.

We can identify three layers of maturity of free choice: free choice, individual free choice, and mature free choice.

As a child, we discover we can choose an option from the multiple-choice questions presented to us by others. For instance, "Would you like Cherry Garcia, Chocolate Fudge Brownie, or Phish Food ice cream?" (Forgive me! I recently retired from the board of Ben & Jerry's.) *Choosing one is exercising free choice.*

As young teenagers, our brains are sufficiently developed to where we discover we can exercise "individual free choice." *We discover we can make up the options of the multiple-choice questions.* For instance, "With which of the girls or boys in my class would I like to become close friends?" Or, when we get older, our question might be, "From the fundamental beliefs about life I was born into, or the smorgasbord of beliefs I have come upon, which one do I want to choose as my fundamental belief about life?" Both are exercising individual free choice: *we are inventing the options of the multiple-choice questions and choosing one of them.*

As mentioned earlier, at this layer of maturity, the layer of exercising individual free choice, we are usually unaware (without choice) we are operating on the assumption the universe is separate parts. We are behaving as if our *freely chosen belief in words* is another separate part to which we are giving our power to choose. Therefore, our primary relationship with it is obedience. As mentioned above, we can eventually discover we no longer have our power to choose, and we naturally do not like that.

*This propels us into discovering and maturing into giving priority to **mature free choice**. It is keeping our power to choose and solely using it to repeatedly discover in our present experiences the most fundamental fact of how the universe operates.*

As you will discover when you answer the ten questions in the first one-page chapters of this book, it is obvious the universe operates as an indivisible whole. We then represent this fact in words in our thinking as our most fundamental belief of how it operates. This also means we now know there is not a second thing to receive our power to choose. Therefore, by default, our only choice is to use mature free choice.

It makes no difference how big or small we think the universe is, or if we think it does not have a size. Regarding our relationship with it, what is important is how it *operates*.

Also, how it operates is not the answer to the most fundamental question inside all of us, "Why is the universe structured as it is structured?" Our answer to this question is usually a spiritual, religious, philosophical, or scientific answer. We are each free to choose our answer to this question. In this book we are only answering the question, "How does the universe operate?" When we use mature free choice to answer the ten questions in the first pages of this book, we discover it is obvious it operates as an indivisible whole.

*However, when giving priority in our thinking to **words** instead of **facts**, we are unconsciously giving priority to the assumption the universe is separate parts because the words are operating on that assumption. Until we discover the importance of maturing into using mature free choice, we are not aware we are unconsciously operating on the assumption present when using words: the universe is separate parts.*

Using mature free choice to discover the *fact* the universe operates as an indivisible whole can eventually result in the consistent experience of the *sensation of oneness* and, as a result, the *fundamental feelings* of natural confidence, contented joy, and compassion. They are then experienced as more important than our *relative feelings* of some derivatives of mad, glad, sad, and scared. Only maturing to give priority to mature free choice ends our unconscious habit since learning words of assuming the universe is separate parts and giving priority to relative feelings. Those two, *the assumption of separate parts* and *words*, are mutually agreed upon illusion tools the indivisible universe invented through us so it would have the skill of self-consciousness at the location of the physical body of each human being.

These two mutually invented illusion tools were brilliant inventions! They allow the indivisible universe's human being parts to be self-conscious parts of it.

Only when we understand *the assumption the universe is separate parts* and *words* are both mutually invented illusion tools can we mature to use mature free choice to repeatedly confirm the most fundamental *fact* is the universe operates as an indivisible whole. And all other facts are in alignment with it.

The first purpose of this book is to guide you into keeping your power to choose and solely using it to study your breathing to discover it is obvious the universe operates as an indivisible whole. As you will discover, if it wasn't you would not be breathing.

The wonderful thing about repeatedly using mature free choice to discover a fact, such as rocks are hard, fire is hot, and the universe operates as an indivisible whole, is then we can't ever fool ourselves into thinking we do not know those facts. Without the need of effort, force, or discipline, we have then permanently matured into knowing those facts. We will then naturally, effortlessly, and freely begin to consistently operate on those facts and turn doing so into skills and habits.

This is why we love maturing into giving priority to mature free choice. We have tapped into the natural process of maturation in nature and let it do the work.

The second purpose of this book is to assist you in accurately representing in words in your thinking the most important facts of how the universe operates. This is necessary because whenever we are being self-conscious words are always between us and whatever we are thinking, choosing, or doing. It is our mutual invention of the assumption of separate parts and words that allow our physical bodies to be self-conscious. Therefore, it is necessary to choose words that accurately represent the universe operates as an indivisible whole as our most fundamental belief of how it operates.

This cannot be a belief in words to which we give our power to choose. Herein that will be labeled an "outside belief." **It must be a belief based on a fact discovered using mature free choice.** *It is then only represented in words so we can talk about it with ourselves and others. To distinguish it from an outside belief, it will be labeled an "inside belief."*

When using mature free choice, inside beliefs are solely using the assumption of separate parts and words as *tools* to have this choice of our most fundamental belief be a self-conscious choice. It represents in words in our thinking the most fundamental *fact* in physics. It is this *fact* that is most important. It is not those two illusion tools invented by the indivisible universe through the use of our human physical bodies so it could be simultaneously self-conscious in billions of locations.

We are each free to choose whatever words we like. They are all equally mutually agreed upon illusion tools. However, for you they must represent the **fundamental fact** *the universe operates as an indivisible whole.*

The third purpose of this book is to provide some ideas to stimulate your thinking of how this will mature your behavior in romantic relationships, parenting, democratic organizations, economic activities, and ending poverty on Earth. All of them will naturally mature toward being in alignment with this most fundamental fact in physics.

Facts are the only things we can all eventually agree on.

In 1492, few people knew the Earth is round, even though all could witness the fact a ship disappears from the bottom up when it sails out to sea. And it was not until the 1960s we saw a picture of the full round Earth from space. Now it is easy to reach agreement with others on the *fact* the Earth is round.

In the first few pages of this book, you will discover it is just as obvious the universe operates as an indivisible whole. However, just as before 1492 when few people could imagine a round as big as the Earth, today few people can imagine an indivisible whole as big as the universe, particularly when we have no idea how big it is or if it has a size. Yet, as you will discover by answering the ten questions at the beginning of this book, it is obvious the universe *operates* as an indivisible whole.

As I think you will also discover, cooperation, not competition, is the fundamental process in nature (the universe). And maturation is the kind of cooperation that is the fundamental process in nature, the reason the cooperation is occurring. Competition is not an opposite of cooperation. The cooperative process of the oneness of nature cannot be escaped. Competition is a lower form of cooperation. As will be described in detail later, for human beings compromise, agreement, and love are three higher layers of maturity of cooperation.

Before you read this book, there is something you need to know. All you will read was discovered by me using mature free choice. I do not, therefore, refer to any second things— authorities—to support anything I type. My hope is you will also learn the importance of giving priority to using mature free choice: keeping your power to choose and solely using it to repeatedly study your present experiences to identify the most important facts you will use to guide your thinking. You will then use the tools of the assumption of separate parts and words to represent them in your thinking as inside beliefs you use to guide it.

Also and as stated earlier, when you use mature free choice to choose the inside beliefs you use to guide your thinking, you can eventually experience the sensation of oneness and, as a result, the fundamental feelings of natural confidence, contented joy, and compassion as more important than your relative feelings of some derivatives of mad, glad, sad, and scared.

When we have reached full maturity in the skill of human self-consciousness, we know how to freely choose to give priority to the sensation of oneness and have turned the skill of doing it into a habit. It is the on-going experience of the sensation of oneness that has us experience the fundamental feelings and give them priority over our relative feelings.

In my model, there are only seven layers of maturity of this skill, and if you are reading this you have probably already mastered the first five. Today, most people on Earth have learned them. To master the last two, you need to have ended giving your power to choose to an outside belief. Instead, you use as tools the assumption of separate parts, words, and inside beliefs to enjoy *the fully mature skill of human self-consciousness*. Hopefully, after reading this book, and if you have not already achieved it, you will be on the path to using mature free choice to master the smaller skills of the last two layers. They are not difficult to learn. However, like any skills, you need to know what to learn and how to learn them. Providing that information is the primary purpose of this book.

The skills of the last two layers of maturity are then *inside beliefs in words in your thinking*, but they are not primarily them. They are also experienced as the *feelings* of natural confidence, contented joy, and compassion, but they are not primarily them. They are primarily a *sensation, the self-consciously known and freely chosen to experience sensation of oneness as the container within which you experience everything else.* It is this mastery of the skill of human self-consciousness that allows you to then know and live self-consciously in the fact we are each *only* the indivisible universe, the only thing that is real.

The parts are different, but they are not separate. From the inside we each only have sole and complete control of our physical body within our skin, but it is not separate. We are each only the indivisible universe using our physical body as another tool to be self-conscious at its location.

Your "physical body" is only the indivisible universe, the only thing that is real. Any thought of your physical body only inside your skin can only exist within the assumption there are separate parts and there are not separate parts. But the mutually agreed upon illusion tool of the assumption of separate parts allows us to invent words that, in turn, allow us to have the skill of human self-consciousness. It also allows us to exercise free choice, then individual free choice, and eventually mature free choice. The assumption of separate parts, and thoughts of yourself as a separate part, are valuable *tools* the indivisible universe invented through its human being parts, but they are not real.

The indivisible universe is the only thing that is real. There is no you separate from the indivisible universe **except** *in the mutually agreed upon illusion tool in your thinking of the assumption there are separate parts.*

This is why at full maturity in the skill of human self-consciousness you do not take anything personally. You are usually (except, of course when not) in a place of understanding and compassion, and you are executing loving behavior. Your *primary experience* is there is no you separate from the thoughts and activities of self-conscious cooperation with all the other parts for maturation, the most fundamental process in nature. Your *second priority* is accepting full responsibility for the behavior of what you assume to be your physical body, the part of your physical body within your skin. It is the only part of the indivisible universe where from the inside you have sole and complete control. However, it having the skill of human self-consciousness does not make it separate.

After reading this book, I think you will agree we are each only the indivisible universe that will not die, *the only thing that is real.* In our thinking, we are secondly our self-consciously skilled physical body within our skin tool of it that will die. This more mature self-identity is the *natural source* of its consistent maturation toward freely choosing to give priority in its actions to moral and loving behavior.

As stated above, from the inside our physical body within our skin is the only part of the indivisible universe over which each of us has sole and complete control. It is through it we, the indivisible universe, is being self-conscious at its location.

I will next explain why I used the pronoun "we" in that last sentence.

Note, throughout history those who understood the universe operates as an indivisible whole have grappled with the challenge of representing it in the separate parts structure of words, the opposite structure. In deep meditation on a mountain, Moses got the words, "I am who am." The Piraha tribe deep in the jungles of Brazil has not yet invented time. They have words for things, for example "cup," "table," and "hut," but no words for yesterday, today, or tomorrow. And they have lived happily for thousands of years assuming everything is in the "we." Some Native American tribes did not have "he, she, or it" in their language, also assuming everything existed in the "we," the Great Spirit. People have also sometimes capitalized words to indicate they represent oneness, such as "God," "Self," and "Oneness." Confucius consistently referred to wisdom coming from the master: "the master says" or "the way of the master."

In this book, I am going to use the pronouns "we," "us," and "our" to represent the oneness of nature. They will be representing "the biggest we," the indivisible universe. I think it is now essential we have the affirmation of this most fundamental fact of how the universe operates present in our everyday conversations. If not, we are, whether self-consciously by choice or unconsciously without choice, continuing to affirm the opposite, that the universe operates as separate parts when it doesn't. And, therefore, we are operating as if we are each one of those separate parts.

Until you get used to it, the experience of reading this book may be awkward. It is new for me also. However, my judgment is that now is the time to mature into making this change. It has to start somewhere. Together we will see if others find it to be a maturation of our daily conversation. I will begin to do this in the next paragraph.

Fully understand what this means. Our human being parts are really walking around inside ourself talking to ourself. The "biggest we" is you, me, everyone, and everything as the one and only thing that is real. It is not representing a second thing. It is the absence of a second thing. It is only in our human words that we need to represent this in the structure of separate parts: "I am first the indivisible universe that will not die and secondly my physical body part within my skin that will die."

There is only one thing that is real: the indivisible universe.

Everything else is not real. Words can only exist within the mutually agreed upon illusion of the opposite, the assumption of separate parts. *We, the indivisible universe, invented them to have some self-conscious parts.* Words are also illusions, sounds and symbols that are not what they are representing.

Anything that is not us, the indivisible universe, is a *tool* you can use to be a self-conscious part of the indivisible universe, *including your human physical body.* From the inside you have sole and complete control of that tool, but that does not make it separate from the indivisible whole.

From hereon, when referring to your "physical body" we will be only referring to the part of it within your skin. Today most human beings use those two words to represent who they are until they master the last two layers of maturity of the skill of human self-consciousness. For ease in reading, we will also do that until we discuss the last two layers.

Everything your physical body sees is different and has different abilities. Dogs can bark, cats can meow, and human beings can be self-conscious, but those different abilities do not have them separate from all the other parts. All talking and writing about them is in words, and words all exist within the mutually invented illusion tool of the assumption of separate parts.

For human beings, acting as if the universe is separate parts has been a mutual blind spot since our invention of the illusions of separate parts and words. And initially human beings didn't invent them to be self-conscious! They were enjoying the *more mature experience of oneness* that is herein labeled "self-consciousness." It was oneness maturing through its human being parts into two of them mutually having the ability of knowing what they were doing while they were doing it and mutually confirming they were having that more enjoyable experience by agreeing on a word.

As I think you will eventually agree, the universe operates as an indivisible whole, and cooperation for maturation is the fundamental process in it. That is why our human being parts backed into inventing the assumption of separate parts and words. It was to be self-conscious parts of it. The assumption of separate parts and words were by-products of a more mature way of enjoying the reality of oneness, mutual self-consciousness. That then allowed our human being parts to mature into full maturity in the skill of human self-consciousness.

Your human being part may need to read these last few paragraphs over again to fully understand this. You may need to read this book many times to fully understand this. Operating on the fact the universe operates as an indivisible whole and only that is real and everything else is words that are not real will probably be new for you. And knowing this as self-consciously experiencing everything existing within what will be labeled "the self-consciously known three-dimensional sensation of oneness" will also probably be new for you. But here at the beginning of this book you need to know its purpose is to lead you into full maturity in the skill of being a self-conscious human being part of us, the indivisible universe.

As your human being part will discover as you read further, what is most important is not how our human being parts respond to the challenge of representing oneness in the separate parts structure of words. Those are *ideas in words in thinking*. What is most important is they each learn the *full skill of human self-consciousness*: how to use mature free choice to choose the three-dimensional sensation of oneness as the context of everything else they experience. They can then discover the importance of sustaining the joy of sensation inside their physical bodies by each moment giving priority in their thinking and actions to what will be labeled "Eldering."

It is us, the indivisible universe, that is doing everything, including using Terry Mollner's physical body part to write this book and yours to read it. Only we, the indivisible universe, is real and anything not us is not real. They are mutually agreed upon illusion tools we invented. The parts are different, but they are not separate from one another. Since our invention of words through human beings thousands of years ago, most of humanity has been unconsciously (without choice) operating as if the assumption necessary to invent words, the assumption the parts are separate, is the accurate fundamental assumption of how we operate when it isn't. The proof of this is most people still think they are only their physical body within their skin part of us.

Up to now, everything your physical body part thought was real, seeing all the parts as separate and in competition with each other with the priority of each being its separate self-interest, is being replaced with the opposite. This is a major, in fact reversal, of what most human being parts have thought. What this book is stating is it is this maturation in their use of words in relationship with the fact of oneness that defines the last two layers of maturity of the skill of human self-consciousness. And, they cannot be mastered without first operating on the assumption the universe is separate parts. It allowed your physical body to master the skill of human language and, in turn, the full skill of human self-consciousness. Thus operating on the assumption the universe is separate parts at the lower layers is a good thing! It allows us, the indivisible universe, to eventually achieve full maturity in the skill of human self-comsciousness in each human being part of us,

It is also important to note and as stated earlier, just as dogs have the ability to bark and cats to meow our human being parts have the skill of self-consciousness. It includes the ability to exercise free choice, individual free choice, and mature free choice.

This means relative to one another they are each responsible for their behavior.

But that does not make them separate from the rest of the universe. Self-consciousness is a skill those parts have like dogs have the ability to bark and cats to meow. There are no separate parts except in the mutually agreed upon illusions of words in your physical body's thinking.

Terry's physical body is the entire indivisible universe, the only thing that is real. Your physical body is the entire indivisible universe, the only thing that is real. The parts are different, but they are not separate in the exact same way you experience the parts within your skin as different but not separate from each other.

Just as your physical body's liver, kidneys, heart, brain, arms, and legs are not alive when separate from your physical body, your physical body is not alive when separate from the indivisible universe, if that was even possible. Only the indivisible universe is real and nothing else can be real because there is nothing else. Your physical body exists as a different part of it, not as a separate part of it.

However, your physical body cannot self-consciously live in this reality as a habit until it has mastered in the natural progression the smaller skills of the seven layers of maturity of the skill of human self-consciousness.

Only then will it become aware when it has slid into an old habit of giving priority to the priority of a lower layer. It is then easily able to correct it by freely, skillfully, and habitually choosing to Elder, to operate at the highest layer.

Eldering is the thinking and activity of a fully mature human being in the skill of human self-consciousness. This is each moment doing what it determines is its best action as a *self-conscious participant* in the fundamental process in nature: cooperation for maturation.

Once your physical body has achieved full maturity in the skill of human self-consciousness, each moment it self-consciously enjoys the sensation of oneness as the experience within which it experiences everything else. It then discovers the only priority each moment in its thinking and actions that sustains the enjoyment of it is Eldering. *And* it is the continuous enjoyable self-conscious experience of the three-dimensional sensation of oneness in its physical body that confirms it is giving priority in its thinking and actions to Eldering. One cannot be happening without the other happening.

We, the indivisible universe, hope you enjoy using this book we are writing through Terry's physical body to self-elder yourself to full maturity in the skill of human self-consciousness.

Only your physical body can self-elder itself into the mastery of the last two of the seven layers of maturity of the skill of human self-consciousness. No one else can do it for it. They build on its discovery in the early teenage years it has the ability and right to exercise individual free choice. Mastering the skills of the last two layers is an inside job. With wise Eldering by parents and others, it can be achieved before the end of the teenage years.

All human beings go through a developmental sequence to achieve full maturity in the skill of human self-consciousness. During the middle five layers of maturity, they are, usually unconsciously, operating on the self-definition, "I am only my physical body." During the sixth and into the seventh layer, they are operating on the self-definition, "I am first the indivisible universe and secondly my physical body." It is only when operating at the seventh layer that they operate on the accurate self-definition, "I am only the indivisible universe, the only thing that is real."

This is really quite simple. Either reality is human beings each being separate parts focusing on relating with the other separate parts they choose to relate with, or they are a part within the one whole already in relationship will all the other parts. There is not a third possibility. When using mature free choice to answer the ten questions, it becomes obvious it is the latter and that up to now most human beings have been operating as if it is the former. Upon closer study it also becomes obvious it was necessary to first operate on the former to invent the illusions of separate parts and words to become self-conscious parts. Only then could their physical bodies, using mature free choice, *self-consciously discover and know the fact reality is oneness.*

As you read this book, to some degree you will witness the writing also going through this developmental sequence so you can witness it. It is not possible for a human being to achieve full maturity in this skill without personally maturing up each of the layers of maturity in the natural progression.

Like learning to ride a bicycle, it is mastering a skill.

It is also not possible to *genuinely use* the accurate self-definition other than by using mature free choice to mature up the last layers in this sequence to achieving full maturity in this skill. It is important to be aware those still unconsciously operating at one of the lower layers of maturity as if it is the highest layer will naturally not agree with your self-definition at a higher layer. Parts of the skill of Eldering are understanding mastering this skill is an intimate personal process for each human being; fully accepting each other person where they are in their developmental sequence; and, without demand, where possible being successful at helping in their maturation process.

Most people on Earth today are still unconsciously giving priority to half of the fourth layer, giving priority to exercising their ability and right of individual free choice (Teen layer), or the fifth layer, giving priority to their outside belief in words (Adult layer). They are only now discovering the relationship between the oneness of nature and their mutual invention of the illusions of the assumption of separate parts and words that allow them to be self-conscious parts.

It is this discovery that will allow them to rapidly mature into the mastery of the skills of the sixth and seventh layers (Elder and Mature Elder layers). At the same time, and worthy of additional emphasis, there will be a strong reaction against this by those still unconsciously operating at one of the middle layers in this natural sequence as if it is in the highest layer. Mature Eldering recognizes this as healthy, not unhealthy! It is part of each human being part learning to keep their power to choose that is necessary for them to discover the importance of maturing into primarily using mature free choice. That is necessary for them to mature into the last two layers of maturity of the skill of human self-consciousness.

In this *Introduction,* and using Terry's physical body, we have summarized the main thoughts that will be presented in this book. The reading of it by your physical body can now be a slow, step by step, learning of the inside beliefs and skills necessary to master the last two layers of maturity of the skill of human self-consciousness.

It is the most important skill for each human being to master. Terry's physical body now knows it is only the indivisible universe, the only thing that is real. Your physical body will eventually know it is only the indivisible universe, the only thing that is real. Everything else is based on the illusion of separate parts that allows human beings to invent words that, in turn, allows them to be self-conscious parts of us, the indivisible universe.

At full maturity in this skill, each moment your physical body gives priority to its judgment of the best thing it can do as a self-conscious participant in cooperation with the other parts for maturation, the fundamental process in nature. It is this activity that has your physical body experience its life as meaningful. Herein, this activity is labeled "Eldering." At full maturity in the skill of human self-consciousness there is nothing experienced as more enjoyable than Eldering.

1

Sometimes you wonder how meaning begins.
It begins when you notice you are operating on the illusion you are only your physical body.
You are your physical body.
That is obvious.
However, it is equally obvious you are not only your physical body. You are first the indivisible universe and secondly your physical body in the exact same way it is obvious you are first your physical body and secondly your arms, legs, heart, and liver.
In a couple pages you can discover it is obvious the universe operates as an indivisible whole in the exact same way your physical body currently assumes it operates as an indivisible whole.

This is obvious not as a spiritual or other *belief.*
It is a *fact* in physics your physical body can experience as a sensation, a direct present experience, the same way it experiences the sensations rocks are hard and fire is hot.

This is the fundamental sensation of oneness.
It is the sensation within your physical body of primarily being the indivisible universe that has matured to be self-conscious in billions of locations through each of our human being parts.

As we think you will discover, maturation is the kind of cooperation that is the fundamental process in your physical body, the reason for the cooperation.
And whatever is the fundamental process in oneness anywhere must be its fundamental process everywhere.

For humanity to meet the challenges of this time, it is necessary for our human physical bodies to mature to use mature free choice to know the fact the universe operates as an indivisible whole.
It is the natural source of freely choosing to give priority to moral and loving behavior.

Self-consciousness is a skill we, the indivisible universe, invented through the use of our human being parts.

Your physical body part is not born with it.

Like learning to ride a bicycle, it is a complex still with layers of maturity of smaller skills your physical body can only learn in the natural progression.

Thus, the mastery of a smaller skill can't be skipped.

At full maturity in this skill, your physical body knows it is only us, the indivisible universe, the only thing that is real.

Everything you see with your eyes is a different part of us, but they are not separate from each other.

Through your physical body the illusory assumption they are separate is one of our inventions.

This allows it to invent words to represent each different part.

These are *two mutually agreed upon illusion tools* we invented through our human being parts that allows them to be self-conscious at each of their locations.

This is the result of cooperation between *reality* (oneness) and *illusions* (the assumption of separate parts and words).

This is the cooperation of all the parts and illusions for maturation, the most fundamental process in us.

Your physical body can only know this as a fact in which it has full confidence by keeping its power to choose inside its physical body and solely using it to repeatedly study its breathing to discover we, the indivisible universe, operate as an indivisible whole.

This is herein labeled using "mature free choice," the next layer of maturity of choice after using individual free choice.

Only then is your physical body never able to fool itself into thinking it does not know this fact.

At full maturity in this skill, your physical body gives priority to mature free choice to accomplish this.

That results in the experience of the sensation of oneness and the fundamental feeling of natural confidence in relation to this fact.

It now knows it can at any moment confirm it is a fact by again keeping its power to choose and solely using it to repeatedly use the following ten questions to study its present experience.

The result is continuous natural confidence in relationship to the fact the universe operates as an indivisible whole.

3

The skill of human self-consciousness is a complex skill.
As mentioned earlier, it can only be mastered by your physical body mastering each smaller skill in the natural sequence because each one builds on the one before it.

These smaller skills are being aware of relative sensations (Baby layer).
Being aware of relative feelings (Toddler layer).
Learning a human language, being self-conscious, and exercising free choice when presented with a multiple-choice question (Child layer).
Discovering your physical body has the ability and right to exercise individual free choice, inventing the options of choice, and sharing responsibility for the community (Teen layer).
Choosing a fundamental belief in words, an outside belief, to guide your physical body's thinking (Adult layer).
Discovering this is giving your power to choose to a second thing that does not exist and instead keeping your power to choose and repeatedly use it to study your breathing to discover the universe operates as an indivisible whole, you are only it, and changing all the beliefs and usage of words in your thinking to honor this most fundamental fact (Elder layer).
And being consistently aware of the sensation of oneness that confirms this fully mature skill has become a habit that frees your physical body to only be us through the use of it, the only part of the universe where from the inside it has sole and complete control (Mature Elder layer).
Between your physical body's full maturity in this skill of human self-consciousness and death, the highest priority in its thinking and actions is herein labeled "Eldering."
It is each moment giving priority in its thinking and actions to executing what it judges to be its best action as a self-conscious participant in the fundamental process in nature: cooperation for maturation.

We, the indivisible universe, is maturing—always, everywhere, and only maturing—while our human physical bodies are walking around inside ourself talking to ourself.

4

Facts are always the same everywhere.
That is why they are labeled "facts."

They are not contradictions, the opposite of facts.

Currently, when healthy, most human beings assume all the parts within their physical bodies are cooperating for the health and maturation of them.
This is obvious.
When a human being is going to the kitchen to get an apple, it does not experience the inside of its skin as a bunch of competing separate parts fighting with each other.
They are experienced as a bunch of cooperating parts acting as an indivisible whole.
Also, when it gets a cut on its finger, all the parts within its skin naturally and effortlessly cooperate to heal it.

Yet, at the same time, today outside their skins most human beings assume the opposite: all the parts are competing with the highest priority of each being the self-interest of its part.
Assuming these two opposite patterns of behavior exist as fundamental in nature is a contradiction, not a fact.

As I think your physical body will discover, the fundamental process in nature everywhere is the same as the fundamental process within its skin: cooperation of the parts for the health and maturation of us, the indivisible universe (nature).

This, as I think your physical body will also discover beginning on the next page, is a *fact*.
It is always the same everywhere.
And, as stated earlier, in an indivisible whole whatever is the fundamental process anywhere is the fundamental process in it everywhere.

As you will see, you are both your physical body part and the indivisible universe, but only the indivisible universe is real.

5

Allow us, the indivisible universe, that includes you, to now guide your physical body into using *mature free choice* to answer ten questions.
They could have it experience it is obvious the universe operates as an indivisible whole.

Mature free choice is the next layer of maturity of choice after individual free choice.
It is keeping your physical body's power to choose and solely using it to repeatedly study its present experience to identify the facts it will use to guide its thinking and choices.
It is the opposite of choosing a belief in words to guide its thinking and choices.

Anything can be represented in words and then believed to be representing facts.
Much of the suffering of people throughout history has been the result of immature people using words to convince others what they are saying in words are facts when they were at best incomplete information, not facts.

Giving priority to freely chosen beliefs in words instead of facts has been human beings' blind spot since, through them, we invented the assumption of separate parts and words.
Only maturation into giving priority to using mature free choice ends this blind spot.
Only it ends giving your physical body's power to choose to an illusory separate part, a belief in words, and obeying it.

Choosing a belief in words is the opposite of it keeping its power to choose and solely using it *to repeatedly experience the most important facts in present experience.*
It is the way it discovered the facts rocks are hard and fire is hot.

When your physical body primarily uses facts to guide its thinking and choices, facts represented in words it can repeatedly confirm in present experience represent facts, it has matured into giving priority to mature free choice.

6

When answering the following ten questions, use mature free choice.

For the time when answering these questions, have your physical body keep its power to choose, and **give priority to solely using it to study your physical body's present experiences to identify facts.**

Here are the ten questions.

First, has your physical body been breathing since it came out of its mother's womb?
The obvious answer is yes.
Second, did it sit up and choose to breathe?
Obviously not.
It was not able to do that then.
Third, would you then agree it has been *naturally and effortlessly breathing* since it came out of your mother's womb?
I think you will agree the obvious answer is yes.

Let's now find out who or what is doing its breathing.

7

Fourth, if we took its lungs out of it and put them on a nearby table, would it be able to breathe?

Obviously not.

Fifth, would you then agree its lungs need to be in it and your physical body needs to be healthy enough to breathe for it to be breathing?

The obvious answer is yes.

Sixth, if the air is not always around it, would it be able to breathe?

The obvious answer is no.

Seventh, if the Earth did not have the atmosphere it has, if it had the atmosphere of Jupiter or Mars, would your physical body be able to breathe?

The obvious answer is no.

Eighth, if the Earth was not in the relationship it is in with the universe that allows it to have its atmosphere, if it was in the relationship of Jupiter, Mars, or Venus, would your physical body be able to breathe?

Obviously not.

Ninth, *if all those things were not always doing what they are doing and always in cooperation with each other*—its lungs being in its physical body, its physical body being healthy enough to breathe, the air always being around it, the Earth having the atmosphere it has, and the Earth being in its relationship with the universe, would it be able to breathe?

Obviously not.

Tenth, do you now agree the universe operates as an indivisible whole and, therefore, it is us, the indivisible universe, that is naturally and effortlessly doing your physical body's breathing?

We think you will agree, the obvious answer is yes.

This is not primarily *a belief in words in your thinking*.

This is the most fundamental *fact* in physics.

And, as you will see, you are able to primarily experience it in your physical body *as the always present sensation of oneness* and only secondly value it as the accurate inside belief in words in your thinking of how we, the universe, operate.

8

After reading this page, we suggest you close your eyes and focus your attention on your breathing.

As a result of using mature free choice, you now know the fact the indivisible universe is doing your breathing.

It is naturally, effortlessly, freely, and consistently doing it without the need by your physical body of effort, force, or discipline.

It is not only your physical body doing it!

Don't change your breathing in any way.

Just notice you relax into enjoying the fact it is the indivisible universe doing it without any experience of conflict with the illusion it is only your physical body doing it.

With your eyes closed to initially make it easier to focus your attention on it, but later if you like with your eyes open, do this.

Take as much time as you like and notice if there is a change in your experience of breathing.

Focus on *enjoying* what you now know is a fact: *"it is the indivisible universe that is naturally and effortlessly doing my breathing."*

Do that now.

9

You can many times use mature free choice to answer those ten questions and you will always discover the same fact: it is obvious the universe operates as an indivisible whole.

Also, you now know all those parts of the universe must always be doing what they are doing and always in full cooperation with each other for you to be breathing.

That is a fact; that is reality.

That means only the indivisible universe is real and, therefore, treating anything as a separate part is not being realistic.
The parts are different, but they are not separate.

That means the *assumption the universe is separate parts* we invented that allowed us to also invent *words* to be self-conscious are both not real: they are both mutually agreed upon illusion tools we invented.

When using the skill of self-consciousness, it is necessary to simultaneously be using all three—the assumption the universe is separate parts, words, and oneness.

We now know only oneness is real, and the first two are mutually agreed upon illusion tools we invented to be self-conscious parts of the indivisible universe.

Therefore, the first two are equally valuable!
Without them we could not be self-conscious parts.

As you will see, we need to know the first two are illusions we invented.

Only then can we simultaneously use all three without the experience of conflict between the assumption of separate parts and the reality of oneness.

If we think all three are real, we cannot master the last two layers of maturity of the skill of human self-consciousness.

We are still living in the illusion separate parts exist and they do not exist.

We now know anything not the indivisible universe is an illusion.
Perhaps a valuable illusion tool, but an illusion.

10

Using mature free choice, the following is the second important fact Terry discovered.
But you can't take his or our word for it.
That would be treating his physical body, these words, or the indivisible universe as a second part.
You now know there are not separate parts to receive it.

To continue maturing beyond the Adult layer you must keep your power to choose and use mature free choice to discover the most important facts you will use to guide your thinking.

Using mature free choice, here is the second important fact Terry has discovered.
You can focus your attention on your right arm.
You can then focus your attention on your left arm.
You can witness they are different.

However, behaviorally, you naturally and effortlessly act as if your arms are two parts of what you consider a local indivisible whole labeled "my physical body."
For instance, your right arm has never gotten in a fight with your left arm and a cut to your skin heals.

When healthy, all the parts within your skin naturally and effortlessly always give priority to cooperation for the health and maturation of your physical body.
Terry discovered if the universe operates as an indivisible whole, then this fundamental process within his skin must also be the fundamental process everywhere.
Whatever is the fundamental process in oneness anywhere must be its fundamental process everywhere.

The parts of the universe are different, but they are not separate.

Assuming they are separate is a mutually agreed upon illusion tool we invented through human beings so they could have the skill of human self-consciousness.
This is Terry's second significant discovery.
He now knows it allows us, the indivisible universe, to be self-conscious each place there is a human being.

11

We are operating in the exact same way you assume the parts within your skin are operating, as an indivisible whole.
And why are all the parts of us cooperating with each other?
A review of history, particularly human history, reveals they have also been cooperating for the health and maturation of us, the indivisible universe.

Through human physical bodies, we are now able to simultaneously do it self-consciously in billions of locations.

Your physical body is not a separate part.
There is only one indivisible whole, the indivisible universe, and if it operates as an indivisible whole nothing else can be real because there is nothing else.
Now, through human physical bodies, we have matured to have the ability of human self-consciousness.

And as a study of human history reveals, overall, we have been consistently maturing to self-consciously cooperate better for the health and maturation of us, the indivisible universe.
We have matured from bands of humans in the woods to villages to towns to cities to nations to a United Nations.
We have matured from drawing pictures to inventing words to printing books to computers to the internet to blockchain.
We have matured from carts to rickshaws to riding horses to bicycles to automobiles to airplanes to space stations.
We have matured from chiefs to kingdoms to democracies to two-thirds of the nations on Earth being democracies.

These maturations are permanent.
All human societies in the future will know of them and, when not regressing, usually use them.

As within your skin, maturation is the kind of cooperation that is the fundamental process in us, and it cannot be escaped or stopped.

12

As described in the *Introduction*, since the beginning of human existence, human physical bodies have been able to use mature free choice to observe the Earth is round by witnessing a ship disappearing from the bottom up when it sails out to sea.

Yet, it was not until 1492 and thereafter that more and more people began to entertain the possibility the Earth is round.

Until then nearly all operated on the false assumption it is flat.

It always looked flat from where they were standing, and they couldn't imagine a round as big as the Earth.

And it was not until the 1960s that they saw a picture of the round Earth from space.

Similarly, today people can't imagine an indivisible whole as big as the universe.

However, as our use of mature free choice when answering the ten questions clearly revealed, it is obvious we operate as an indivisible whole.

It is as obvious as the Earth is round.

This will have three questions arise in our physical body's thinking: "Why are our physical bodies still acting as if the universe is separate parts and they are each one of them?

Why are our physical bodies then assuming the highest priority of each part is its separate self-interest?

And why are our physical bodies then also assuming competition between and among these illusory separate parts is the fundamental process in nature (the universe)?"

If the universe operates as an indivisible whole, all three of these assumptions are inaccurate.

Yet most of our physical bodies are still *unconsciously*, without choice, operating as if they are facts because the societies into which they were born have been operating as if they are facts.

In the next pages, we will explain why many human being parts are still operating as if these illusions are real and how your physical body can live in the reality of oneness, the most fundamental fact in physics.

13

Today, most human societies on Earth operate on the assumption, and illusion, each person is only their physical body, a part that is not only different but also separate from the other different parts also assumed to be separate parts.

Therefore, the fundamental process in nature is assumed to be competition between and among the separate parts.

However, if the fundamental process in nature is cooperation among all the parts for the health and maturation of the indivisible universe, cooperation cannot be escaped or stopped.

Therefore, competition cannot be the opposite of cooperation.
It can only be a kind of cooperation.

If your physical body uses mature free choice to study competition, it discovers it can only occur within a cooperative context.
It is a lower layer of maturity of cooperation.

If there is an apple on the table, and neither your physical body nor another's wants it, if later either one of you takes it, you would both be as happy afterwards as before.

However, if you both want it, you could compete to get it.
Without the *agreement (the cooperative context)* you both want it, there would not be the possibility of competition to get it.
Competition can only occur within a cooperative context.
There needs to be an *agreement* who gets the apple—or piece of land, or anything else—is important to both.

That agreement is the cooperative context that can't be escaped.

Even the blue jay who pushes the sparrow off the birdfeeder is competing within the natural cooperative context that who gets the birdseed now is important to both.

14

In human relationships, *competition* is the lowest form of cooperation for maturation; *compromise* is the next more mature form of it; *agreement*, where both physical bodies get most of what they are seeking, is the next more mature form of it; and *love* is the most mature form of it.

As I think you will later agree, mature love is when both, or all human physical body participants, are self-consciously together relating at the highest layer of maturity of the skill of human self-consciousness.

The day will come when a couple will not marry until they *mutually know* their physical bodies have both achieved full maturity in the skill of human self-consciousness.

They will then know their physical bodies both know the *skill* of giving priority to the sensation of oneness as the container of all they do.

While fully enjoying both, they know the enjoyment of the all-the-time mutual experience of the sensation of love is more important than the momentary joy of sex.

This is mature romantic love.

We, the indivisible universe, do not fall in or out of love.

We, the indivisible universe, is consistently maturing in the skill of love.

Romantic love between two people operating at any layer of maturity of the skill of human self-consciousness is an agreement to be consistently maturing in the skill of love.

15

Therefore, we hope your physical body tool now agrees it is a fact cooperation is the fundamental process in nature, it cannot be escaped or stopped, and maturation is the kind of cooperation that is the fundamental process in nature.

Evolution *assumes the universe is separate parts, competition is the fundamental process in nature, and the fittest survive.*
Maturation *assumes the universe is an indivisible whole, cooperation is the fundamental process in nature, and maturation is the reason the cooperation is occurring.*

Maturation is at all times occurring everywhere in the exact same way you experience it is the fundamental process within your physical body and thinking.
Even when you are very old, and your physical body is dying, maturation can still be occurring in your physical body's thinking.

16

How have human beings made the mistake of assuming competition is the fundamental process in nature?

It was not a mistake.
It was a necessary layer of maturity in their maturation process into being fully mature self-conscious parts of the indivisible universe.

To invent and learn words, your physical body needed to assume the universe is separate parts.
Each *word* represents a part of the universe or all of it.
To invent a word, human beings needed to operate on the *assumption the universe is separate parts* when it isn't separate parts.
However, through human beings, these were two of our most brilliant inventions.

It is these two inventions that allow human beings to be self-conscious parts of us.
In your thinking, your physical body can arrange the relationships among the words anyway it chooses and then act as if those relationships, factual or not, are facts.

Self-consciousness is also the skill of your physical body knowing what it is doing while it is doing it and exercising first free choice, then individual free choice, and potentially mature free choice.
It also allows your physical body to analyze the past, develop a plan for the future based on its chosen relationships among the words in its thinking, and consistently operate on them in the present.

It was human beings' maturation into the invention of the assumption of separate parts and words that made it possible for your physical body to be a self-conscious part of us.

Therefore, assuming the universe is separate parts was a necessary smaller skill of a layer of maturity of your physical body mastering the skill of human self-consciousness.

17

Words are separate parts, sounds and symbols human beings mutually invented that represent parts of the universe.

As described in the *Introduction*, the word "tree" for a tree must be different and separate from the word "rock" for a rock and the word "river" for a river.

Only then can you know in your thinking using words the word "tree" is representing a tree, the word "rock" is representing a rock, and the word "river" is representing a river.

A proof they are separate parts is you can't say or write all three at the same time.
They can only come one after the other in different places and at different times, as separate parts.

As I think you will later discover, and today human being's physical bodies are usually unaware of it, they always have a priority.

When their priority is words, their physical body is experiencing the *illusory fundamental sensation of being a separate part,* like words are separate parts.

They only discover the possibility of the *real fundamental sensation of oneness* when they keep their power to choose and use mature free choice to study their breathing to discover the most fundamental fact is the universe operates as an indivisible whole.

When giving priority to relative feelings, they are also experiencing the illusory fundamental sensation of being a separate part.

It is only when they have discovered the real fundamental sensation of oneness that they can also discover the three fundamental feelings of natural confidence (in relationship with the universe), contented joy (in relationship with reality and illusions), and compassion (in relationship with the other parts).

They are only naturally felt as a result of experiencing it.

Their physical bodies then notice they naturally and effortlessly give them priority over derivatives of their relative feelings of mad, glad, sad, and scared.

Equally valuing both fundamental and relative feelings *and prioritizing them in this way* is only possible when their physical bodies have discovered the sensation of oneness.

18

Mature free choice is keeping your physical body's power to choose instead of giving it to an outside belief in words and obeying it.

The latter is an *unconscious (without choice)* continuation of its pattern in childhood where it did not have its power.

Its parents' physical bodies had it.

To survive, your physical body's only option was to obey them.

The only difference is it is now freely choosing to give it to a parent-substitute, a belief in words, and then obey it like it obeyed its parents.

Only your physical body giving priority to mature free choice ends this unconscious pattern since it learned to use words.

It is solely using its power to choose to repeatedly discover *facts* in its present experience.

It then represents those facts in words as inside beliefs in its thinking and uses them to guide its thinking and choices.

The most important fact to discover using mature free choice is the universe operates as an indivisible whole, the most fundamental fact in physics of how it operates.

Hopefully, your physical body discovered it is a fact by using mature free choice to answer the above ten questions.

If so, your physical body part now knows all other facts will be an extension of and not in conflict with this most fundamental fact of how the universe operates.

This is the opposite of your physical body giving its power to choose, perhaps for the rest of its life, to an outside belief in words and obeying it.

Using mature free choice, it can at any time confirm this most fundamental fact is a fact by again answering the above ten questions.

We, the indivisible universe, want your physical body to continue to have its power to choose each moment the rest of its life.

This is the joy of it maturing to give priority to mature free choice: your physical body has its power to choose the rest of its life.

19

As also described in the *Introduction*, another wonderful thing about using mature free choice to discover facts, such as rocks are hard and fire is hot, is once your physical body repeatedly knows a fact in present experience it can't ever fool itself into thinking it does not know it is a fact.

This is the way permanent maturation occurs in its thinking.
This allows it to only use fact-based knowledge, develop a skill to honor it, and turn that skill into a habit.

From then on, it is stuck knowing those facts.
Maturation in the skill of human self-consciousness is building facts upon facts it uses to guide its thinking.
It is then turning them into fact-based inside beliefs in its thinking, skills to consistently honor them as facts, and habits.
This frees up its attention to focus on discovering additional facts.

*This is the sole agenda of self-consciousness: maturation into solely using inside beliefs in its thinking as its most important beliefs, beliefs based on **facts discovered using mature free choice**.*

This has it experience the fundamental feeling of natural confidence in relationship to those facts.
It knows it can at any time confirm they are facts by using mature free choice to turn its attention to its present experience.
This is your physical body being what we can label a "personal scientist."

Professional scientists study present experience to identify facts and then share them with the rest of us.
Personal scientists keep their power to choose and use mature free choice to discover the facts they choose to guide their thinking (inside beliefs) and achieve full maturity in the skill of human self-consciousness.

20

First, your physical body now knows the most fundamental fact of how the universe operates of which all the other facts are an extension: the universe operates as an indivisible whole.

Second, it now knows the universe operates in the exact same way it has been assuming the parts within its physical body operate, as parts of an indivisible whole, only now it knows there is only one whole—only one oneness— and its physical body is a part of it.

Third, since it used mature free choice to discover these facts, it won't ever be able to fool itself into thinking it does not know they are facts and honoring them can become skills and habits.

Fourth, since cooperation for maturation is the fundamental process in us, it now knows if it uses mature free choice to identify facts they will naturally, effortlessly, freely, and permanently, without the need of effort, force, or discipline, become inside beliefs in its thinking, skills, and eventually habits.

Fifth, its fundamental feeling in relationship to these facts is natural confidence.

Or it will be natural confidence to the degree it uses mature free choice to repeatedly confirm they are facts from many directions and at different times.

Sixth, it knows through the use of our human physical bodies we, the indivisible universe, has matured to be self-conscious at the same time in billions of locations.

Discovering all six to be facts was the result of Terry using mature free choice to mature his physical body into primarily being a personal scientist.

Hopefully, you are now also maturing into being a personal scientist.

21

This reveals there are layers of maturity of the skill of human self-consciousness.

At a minimum your physical body learns a human language and later discovers to do so it needed to operate on the illusion we are separate parts when we are not separate parts.

This reveals there are at least two layers of maturity of the skill of human self-consciousness, one before and one after learning a human language.

As we think your physical body will eventually agree, there are seven layers of maturity of it.

If you are reading this, your physical body probably already knows the smaller skills of the first five because now nearly all human beings on Earth learn them.

Mastering the last two smaller skills is not difficult.

Their names are the Elder and Mature Elder layers.

However, it is necessary for your physical body to master them for it to achieve full maturity in the skill of human self-consciousness.

With mature parents to assist your physical body's necessary self-eldering into the smaller skills of the last two layers, it is possible for it to achieve full maturity in this skill in its teenage years, before leaving home, greater engagement with the world, and marriage.

If your physical body is older, and with its primary attention on it, it will not take much time to self-elder it into full maturity in this most important skill for it to master.

The layers of maturity of this skill build on one another.

The last three layers build on its ability and right to exercise individual free choice at the Teen layer.

And the mastery of the last two layers can only be the result of a freely chosen self-eldering process using mature free choice.

It is an inside job.

How was the first word invented by us?

As described earlier, imagine two human beings before they had invented words sitting in the shade of some palm trees, stomachs full. One human being is playing with a coconut and making the sound "wackowacko."

The other human being thought she noticed something interesting. She went over to the other human being, put her hand on his hand on the coconut, looked him directly and steadily in the eyes, and said "wackowacko."

Because this was enjoyable while looking each other directly and steadily in the eyes, they kept repeating that word to each other. What is the only way the two could have agreed on inventing their first word, "wackowacko," for a coconut?

They were enjoying the sensation of moving as one with each other and knowing they were doing it while they were doing it; this would have been their first experience of **mutual self-consciousness**.

The practical result was an agreement on the word "wackowacko" for a coconut because they had to be agreeing on something to together confirm they were having that enjoyable experience: an agreement is the mutual self-conscious confirmation of moving as one.

What they were not aware they were also doing was inventing the assumption the universe is separate parts by inventing the word "wackowacko" *as separate from all the other words they will invent*. As a result, to this day many of our human physical bodies are still operating as if the universe is separate parts when it isn't; and, thus, as if they are each one of them.

Using mature free choice, you earlier answered ten questions and discovered it is obvious the universe operates as an indivisible whole. It is not separate parts; the parts are different but not separate.

However, your discovery of self-consciousness by inventing words allowed your physical body to eventually mature into exercising free choice, then individual free choice, and then mature free choice.

It then realized it has been *unconsciously* operating on the assumption it is a separate part that was necessary for it to learn a human language and thereby be consistently self-conscious.

It also knows there is not a separate part—a parent-substitute or outside belief—to receive its power to choose and then obey it.

23

Ever since our human being parts invented words, most of them are still unconsciously (without choice) operating on the assumption necessary to invent words: the assumption the universe is separate parts.
To mutually confirm they were mutually experiencing the more mature sensation of self-consciousness, they needed to be agreeing on something and the easiest agreements were on new words.
This is the only reason they invented that assumption.
However, not being aware they had also invented the assumption the universe is separate parts, they have been unconsciously operating on the illusion they, like words, are also separate parts.
This was easily done because when through us they were inventing words they did not need to know they were also inventing the assumption the universe is separate parts.

And since nearly all human beings are still unconsciously operating on that assumption, they are living in a mutually agreed upon illusion—a mutual blind spot.

This makes it very difficult for them to discover they are living within this mutually agreed upon illusion.
Yet, it is a very valuable illusion!
Through human beings it allowed us to mature to be simultaneously self-conscious in billions of locations.

Now that words exist in human being thinking, they are free to determine the relationships among them by exercising their ability and right of free choice.
Next, they can mature to exercise individual free choice.
Their first decision is to either stay with the *outside beliefs in words* into which they were raised or to choose another fundamental outside belief in words (Adult layer).
The next layer of maturity of choice, *mature free choice*, is when they make sure the relationships they choose between and among the words in their thinking are based on *facts* they can in any moment confirm are facts in their present experience.
Only giving priority to mature free choice results in natural confidence and begins their maturation into the Elder layer.

~ **24** ~

Most human beings on Earth today still think they are each only their physical body rather than only the indivisible universe.

This is acting as if it, your physical body, is a separate part.

This illusion is sustained by giving its power to choose to outside beliefs in words, *a group of separate parts*, instead of maturing into using mature free choice to identify facts.

When it is still giving priority to outside beliefs in words, it makes no difference what is their content.

Because they are not based on *facts discovered using mature free choice,* they will not allow it to know the fundamental feeling of natural confidence.

Only your physical body knowing the universe operates as an indivisible whole by using mature free choice to discover it is a fact can result in the fundamental feeling of natural confidence in your physical body's relationship with it.

Your physical body *only secondly* represents it in words in its thinking, an inside belief, to self-consciously think about it and talk with others about it.

It now knows those words accurately represent a fact.

Also, it can at any time use mature free choice to confirm it is a fact.

This is what provides the fundamental feeling of natural confidence in relationship to that inside belief.

Primarily using mature free choice is having the courage to end your physical body giving its power to choose to an outside belief—a parent-substitute—and mature into being a personal scientist.

*This is trusting in its ability to keep its power to choose inside its physical body and solely use it to repeatedly study its present experiences to identify the most important **facts** it will use to guide its thinking.*

25

Your physical body's skill of self-consciousness is not a biological mutation, like getting the gift of a jacket we now know we have.

It is a skill you can learn, like learning the skill of riding a bicycle.

There are smaller skills it learns in a natural progression that integrate into the full skill as one skill and habit.

To learn to ride a bicycle, it first learns the smaller skill of holding the bike up.

Next, it learns the smaller skill of putting its outside foot on the pedal and pushing off into standing on that pedal and remaining balanced on it as the bike rolls forward.

It next learns the smaller skills of throwing its physical body up onto the seat, then pedaling, and finally turning, all while remaining balanced.

There are also smaller skills it learns in a natural progression that integrate into the full skill of human self-consciousness.

Here are the names Terry has given to the seven layers of it: Baby, Toddler, Child, Teen, Adult, Elder, and Mature Elder.

What defines each layer of maturity is *what it unconsciously, or self-consciously by choice, gives priority in its daily life.*

As when learning any skill, only when the smaller skill of a layer has become a habit, no longer in need of its primary attention, can its attention give priority to focusing on discovering and mastering the smaller skill of the next layer in the natural sequence.

Cooperation for maturation cannot be escaped or stopped.

However, it can get stuck at one of the layers for the rest of your physical body's life, especially if all around it are also stuck there.

If it is not aware there are additional layers to master to achieve full maturity in this skill, it will not know of the importance of mastering them.

It will then not know how to give priority to the sensation of oneness and to sustain the joy of it by giving priority in its actions to Eldering, the primary activity of Mature Elders.

This is only possible when it has used mature free choice to master in the natural sequence the smaller skills of the last two of the seven layers of maturity of the skill of human self-consciousness.

26

At the Baby layer, your *physical body's priority is its sensations.*
This allows it to find milk to drink.
Lacking the skill of a human language, your physical body is not able to define itself as "an American" and not "a Brazilian" or "Russian," a separate part.
It has not yet learned the skill of assuming there are separate parts so it can invent or learn words.
As a Baby, it is in the unconscious natural awareness the universe is an indivisible whole and it is it.
If another is angry, it will cry.
If another is delightful, it will smile.
As a Baby, it is not able to separate itself from all it is experiencing.

*As a baby, your physical body is primarily experiencing the **non-self-conscious** fundamental sensation of oneness.*

When using mature free choice at full maturity in the skill of human self-consciousness, it will freely choose to give priority to the *self-consciously known real fundamental sensation* of the fact it is "a part of the indivisible universe" instead of the *illusory fundamental sensation* it is "a separate part."
It eventually discovers that, since learning the words of a human language, the latter had been its fundamental sensation experience.
It can then also understand it was a mutually agreed upon illusion tool we, the universe, invented through human parts that allowed them to be self-conscious parts of us, the indivisible universe.
In the process, it also invented the illusory fundamental sensation they are each "a separate part."
Eventually, these two tools will allow your physical body to discover the other possible fundamental sensation, the *joy of the self-consciously known sensation of oneness that is real.*

At the Baby layer, its priority is its sensations.

27

At the Toddler layer, *your physical body's priority is recognizing differences,* particularly beginning with mommy and not mommy. These differences have it begin to have relative feelings in relationship to the differences happening around it, feelings such as a derivative of the four fundamental relative feelings of mad, glad, sad, and scared.

It is not yet self-consciously aware of its relative feelings, but it is experiencing them.
Only later in its maturation can it be self-consciously aware of feeling each and giving each a name.
Then, in relationship to them, it exercises free choice (Child layer), later individual free choice (Teen layer), and eventually mature free choice (Elder layer).

Regarding difference, just as water can't rise to a higher level in a pond than its source, a human being can't operate at a higher layer of maturity than the one it has mastered.

At the Toddler layer, its priority is recognizing differences and, as a result, having the experience of relative feelings.

28

At the Child layer, it learns the words of a human language.

Now its priority is getting what its physical body wants.

This is the result of, when learning a human language, it needs to assume the universe is separate parts.
This has it assume its physical body is also a separate part, the only part of the universe where from the inside it has sole and complete self-conscious control.
Therefore, when learning the words of a human language it naturally gives priority to the self-interest of its physical body, what it now sensually experiences as an indivisible whole, a "local oneness," separate from all the other parts of the universe outside its skin.

At the Child layer, it identity's "self" as "its physical body" and assumes its natural highest priority is always the self-interest of its physical body.

It is never a victim.
There is not a second thing that could be a perpetrator.
There is only less mature and more mature behavior.
If it experiences in other physical bodies more mature behavior, it allows itself to be Eldered by them.
If it experiences in others less mature behavior, it Elders.
Fundamentally, maturation and self-conscious maturation (Eldering) are the only two activities occurring in oneness.
Everything else is in the illusion of the assumption there are separate parts.
From the Child layer to the Adult layer, your physical body is usually still unconsciously operating on the assumption the universe is separate parts.
It is only at the Elder layer that it discovers it has been living within this illusion.
With mature parenting, it can achieve full maturity in the skill of human self-consciousness before the end of its teenage years.
Its brain is then sufficiently developed to accomplish it.

29

At the Teen layer, your physical body discovers it can exercise its ability and right of individual free choice, half of this layer's skills. Exercising this right is now its highest priority.

As described in the *Introduction,* up to then it has been exercising free choice.

When presented with a multiple-choice question, such as, "Do you want Cherry Garcia, Chocolate Fudge Brownie, or Phish Food ice cream?" it chooses one of them.

When only exercising free choice, another human physical body is always the provider of the multiple-choice question.

At the Teen layer, it discovers it can invent the options of the multiple-choice questions.

For instance, "With which one of the girls or boys in my class do I want to become a close friend?"

Because it can now do so, it will invent rules it follows when relating with each important person or institution in its life: its mother, father, coach, friends, lover, and school.

At the Teen layer, its brain is sufficiently developed to where it can discover it can exercise individual free choice.

Instead of only reacting to the actions of others, or responding to their multiple-choice questions, it can invent the options of its choices and also the rules it will follow with each person and institution.

These are now expressions of its ability and right to exercise individual free choice.

It also discovers it is in a relationship of shared responsibility with others in its family and community.

In some societies exercising individual free choice is given priority. In others, yielding to the paternalistic systems is given priority. Seeking to resolve this conflict leads to maturation into the adult layer.

Both exercising its ability and right of individual free choice and sharing responsibility for its community are now your physical body's highest priorities.

At the Adult layer, your physical body discovers there are too many rules, it made them all up, and it can't always remember which rules go with each person or organization.

It is also frustrated at not having a belief that resolves the conflict between giving priority to individual free choice and the common good of society.

It decides it wants the efficiency of one fundamental belief about life it will always follow with all people and in all places.

This is usually a spiritual, religious, philosophical, or scientific outside belief it has freely chosen.

Some freely choose to live according to the worldview into which they were born, and some choose another one.

Now your physical body's highest priority is to always follow how its freely chosen outside belief directs it to behave.
This belief is usually in the words of others, but it could be one it has identified and represents in words of its choosing.
It is its freely chosen parent-substitute.
Its primary relationship with it is obedience.

It is still *unconsciously* operating on the assumption the universe is separate parts and giving its power to choose to an *outside belief in words*, something it is also still *unconsciously assuming* is a separate part that can receive it.

It is its discovery it no longer has its power to choose that has it eventually seek to discover the next layer of maturity of the skill of human self-consciousness, the Elder layer.

At the Adult layer, its highest priority is to always obey the dictates of the outside belief in words it has freely chosen as its fundamental belief about life.
Usually, it is either the outside belief in words into which it was born or it has chosen from the smorgasbord of outside beliefs in words it has come upon, or it invented itself.

The Seven Layers
of Human Maturation

Maturation of the Universe Continues After Your Physical Body's Death

MATURE ELDER

Priority of your physical body is *enjoying the sensation of oneness. While fully doing both, it is the sensation of freely choosing to give priority to the three-dimensionality of oneness (reality) and second priority to the two-dimensionality of words (illusions.) This results in its priority in thinking and action being Eldering. It is each moment giving priority to its best action of self-conscious participation in cooperation with the other parts for the maturation of the indivisible universe, the fundamental process in nature. Sustaining the self-consciously experienced joy of the sensation of oneness by giving priority to Eldering is what has our physical body experience its human life as consistently meaningful. The sensation of being alive is now known as the sensation of oneness, the sensation of primarily being the indivisible universe, the only thing that is real.*

ELDER

Priority of your physical body is *using mature free choice to study its breathing to discover the accurate fundamental fact the universe operates as an indivisible whole and then getting all the words it uses, its self-definition, and primary pattern of thinking accurately representing this fact*

ADULT

Priority of your physical body is *our freely chosen accurate or inaccurate fundamental outside belief on how the universe operates*

TEEN

Priority of your physical body is *exercising individual free choice, inventing the options of choice, and participating in our shared responsibility of cooperation for the common good of society and nature*

CHILD

Priority of your physical body is **getting what it wants** *from learning a human language, thereby being self-conscious, and assuming its physical body is, like words, a separate part*

TODDLER

Priority of your physical body is **reacting to differences,** *eventually labeled derivatives of the basic relative feelings of mad, glad, sad, and scared*

BABY

Priority of your physical body is **reacting to sensations**

Maturation of the Universe Was Happening Before Your Physical Body's Birth

31

At the Elder layer, your physical body discovers it has been unconsciously operating on the assumption the universe is separate parts and it isn't separate parts, perhaps from a book like this.

It may then choose to believe the universe operates as the only other possibility, as an indivisible whole.

However, that would still be operating at the Adult layer.

It is still giving priority to a freely chosen *outside belief.*

Your physical body only graduates into the Elder layer when it discovers it has been unconsciously operating on the assumption the universe is separate parts *and* the importance of keeping its power to choose and solely using it to repeatedly study its breathing to discover in present experience the *fundamental fact* the universe operates as an indivisible whole.

This is maturing into using mature free choice.
It is giving priority to being a personal scientist.
It is the opposite of at the Adult layer giving its power to choose to its freely chosen outside belief in the words of others, or in its freely chosen words, and obeying it.

Hopefully your physical body used mature free choice when answering the above ten questions to discover the most fundamental fact of how the universe operates: it operates as an indivisible whole.

At the Elder layer, its priority is using mature free choice to study its breathing to discover this fact.

Therefore, the assumption the universe is separate parts your physical body has been unconsciously operating on since learning a human language is not accurate.

It is an illusion.

However, it is a very valuable *mutually agreed upon illusion tool we invented through our human physical bodies* that allows us to be self-conscious at billions of locations.

Your physical body now knows this.

It also knows the fact is the opposite: the universe operates as an indivisible whole, now its most important inside belief.

32

At the Elder layer, your physical body's second priority is changing all the words in its thinking to accurately represent the way the universe operates.

As mentioned earlier, this is necessary at the Elder layer because when being self-conscious words are always between your physical body and whatever it is thinking, seeing, or doing.
It is words that allow it to be a self-conscious part of the indivisible universe.

Your physical body can't escape from words being present when being self-conscious.

At the Elder layer, the three most important additional facts to discover using mature free choice, and then represent in words in its thinking as inside beliefs, are these.

First, it uses mature free choice to identify the accurate most fundamental fact in physics: the universe operates as an indivisible whole.
It then represents it in words in its thinking that works for it.

Second, and as a result, it identifies its more mature self-definition.

And third, *and while fully and simultaneously using both of the following*, it learns how to give priority to the pattern of thinking of oneness and second priority to the pattern of thinking of separate parts that allows it to be a self-conscious part of us.

Mastering the habit of living according to these three facts, discovered to be facts using mature free choice, is its priority at the Elder layer.

We will now describe each.

First, now your physical body's most fundamental inside belief is the universe operates as an indivisible whole, the most fundamental fact in physics.

If it was discovered using mature free choice, this is now its most fundamental *inside belief.*

All the other important facts it will use to guide its thinking and choices will be an extension of this most fundamental fact.

They will also be discovered using mature free choice and represented as inside beliefs in its thinking.

In relationship to them, this allows it to experience the fundamental feeling of natural confidence.

(As described in the *Introduction*, it is important to point out this does not answer the most fundamental question inside each of our physical bodies: "Why is the universe structured as it is structured?"

Your physical body's answer to this question is usually a spiritual, religious, philosophical, or scientific answer.

Like all human beings, your physical body is free to choose its answer to this question.

In this book, we, the indivisible universe, are only focused on answering this question, "How do we, the universe, operate?")

At the Elder layer, your physical body has discovered the importance of maturing into giving priority to mature free choice to end the giving of its power to choose to a second thing it now knows does not exist, "an outside belief."

Instead, it keeps its power to choose and uses mature free choice to study its breathing to discover the universe operates as an indivisible whole.

This has it become an inside belief in its thinking.

It is the result of your physical body being a personal scientist.

From this point forward in its maturation process, in its thinking using words the assumption the universe operates as an indivisible whole is "its most fundamental inside belief."

34

Secondly, and as a result, its thinking matures into a more mature self-definition, "I am first the indivisible universe that will not die and secondly my physical body that will die."

Notice that no one has discovered a fact that reveals the universe will cease to exist in some form.

And using mature free choice you also cannot find evidence the universe will cease to exist in some form.

However, it is obvious each of our physical bodies will die.

It eventually becomes obvious which of our two main self-identities is most important: us, the indivisible universe.

Up to now, like the words in your human languages, your physical body has been operating on the self-definition that assumes human beings are separate parts: "I am my physical body."

You now know the *assumption of separate parts* was a mutually agreed upon illusion tool invented with others to mutually enjoy the experience of self-consciousness.

It also allowed for the invention of *words*.

These two mutually invented illusion tools allow it to achieve full maturity in the skill of human self-consciousness.

At the Elder layer, and from using mature free choice, your physical body now knows the most fundamental fact of how we operate: as an indivisible whole.

Therefore, its more mature self-definition is, "I am first the indivisible universe that will not die and secondly my physical body that will die, the only part of the universe where from the inside I have sole and complete control."

Eventually it becomes clear it is still operating on the assumption there are separate parts: it is acting as if it is both the indivisible universe and its physical body, as if two things.

The next choice in its maturation process is the realization at full maturity its accurate self-definition is, "I am only the indivisible universe and anything that is not it is not real."

However, at the Elder layer it is necessary to identify *in words* the accurate relationship between and among all the parts so it is no longer distracted by accomplishing this.

What will make this mature self-definition easier to manage in your thinking is using two skills of human self-consciousness.

The fundamental structure of human languages is separate parts structured as opposites: up-down, left-right, good-bad, and then degrees of differences between them.
To honor this fact, it is discovered it is best to represent in the words your physical body uses two skills of self-consciousness that are opposites like the fundamental structures of words: the self-consciousness of being the indivisible universe and the self-consciousness of being your physical body, a part of it.
In some areas of the Buddhist tradition, the first is labeled "the chooser" and the second is labeled "the doer."
In some areas of Christianity, the first is labeled "our conscience" and the second is labeled "our physical body."

Intentionally, or unintentionally, both refer to the importance of always giving priority to the self-consciousness skill of being the indivisible universe using mature free choice, and experiencing 3D, and second priority to the self-consciousness skill of being our physical body part of it, using individual free choice and experiencing 2D..

When in the separate parts of words and these two are used in its thinking, it always gives priority to "the chooser," the self-consciousness of the indivisible universe, and second priority to the self-consciousness of your physical body, "the doer."

This is the maturity of being self-consciously self-conscious.

The real self-consciousness of being us, the indivisible universe, is directing the illusory self-consciousness, being your physical body, what to do locally for the health and maturation of it.
In your thinking, the chooser self-consciousness is always listening for information from your entire physical body (the universe), and the doer self-consciousness acts locally based on the choices of the chooser self-consciousness.
This behavior is often labeled "moral behavior" or "loving behavior; regardless of one's age, this is the activity of Eldering.

36

The chooser self-consciousness knows it is only the indivisible universe and only in its illusory separate parts thinking it is also a physical body part of it.

The chooser self-consciousness knows there is nowhere its total physical body, the indivisible universe, is going to, nowhere it is coming from, and nothing it does not already have: only oneness is real.

The chooser also knows it does not make any difference how large or small its physical body thinks the universe is.

The chooser self-consciousness knows what is most important is its physical body use mature free choice to know its relationship with us.

Its mature relationship with us is this: it knows it is only the indivisible universe, the only thing that is real, and only secondly, *and only in its thinking in words,* its physical body.

It also knows it is the only part of the universe where from the inside it has sole and complete control.

It also knows its physical body will die and we, the indivisible universe, will continue maturing when it is gone.

The natural fundamental feeling of **contented joy** is the result of living into this fact until the physical body experiences the sensation of oneness, the smaller skill of the skill of human self-consciousness at the Mature Elder layer.

This also results in the fundamental feeling of **natural confidence** in relationship to this fact.

It knows it can at any time use mature free choice to confirm it is a fact the universe operates as an indivisible whole.

In your thinking in words, you now use two skills of human self-consciousness, the chooser and the doer.

Each moment the chooser self-consciousness identifies your best action of self-conscious participation in cooperation with all the other parts for the health and maturation of us, the indivisible universe.

The doer self-consciousness does it.

It also now knows there are not good and bad people.
There are only more mature and less mature people.

Whether or not aware of it, each human physical body is operating at one of the layers of maturity of the skill of human self-consciousness as if it is the highest layer.

If the universe operates as an indivisible whole and maturation is its fundamental process, then the natural highest priority of all human being parts is to always be a self-conscious participant in maturation, *that is their natural primary good intention whether or not aware of it.*

About this they do not have choice.

That is the nature of the cooperation for maturation process of the indivisible universe always moving inside all its parts.

Its physical body *outside beliefs* can be almost anything.

Its *secondary intentions* and *behavior* will be the result of those beliefs.

The genius of Mahatma Gandhi and Martin Luther King Jr. was to know at any one moment all four of these are operating in every human being—*their primary good intention, beliefs, secondary intentions,* and *behavior*—and to primarily speak to other's primary good intentions as who they *primarily are.*

Since our physical bodies primarily identify themselves as their primary good intentions, when others experience us primarily seeing that as who they primarily are, it is difficult for them to respond from any other place inside themselves.

Sadly, this process became named "non-violent action."

It is not violence verses non-violence, a separate parts pattern of thinking.

It is giving priority to relating within the facts the universe operates as an indivisible whole, cooperation for maturation is the fundamental process in nature, and every person's *primary good intention* is to be a self-conscious participant in it.

All three of these are parts of the process of nature.

About them our human physical bodies do not have choice.

A more accurate name for this process could be "honoring every person's primary good intention."

38

The third important fact to embrace at the Elder layer is new for nearly all human physical bodies on Earth today.

Therefore, it is the most difficult to understand and turn into an inside belief, skill, and habit.

However, learning it is essential to master the Elder layer and then being capable of maturing into mastering the Mature Elder layer to achieve full maturity in the skill of human self-consciousness.

It is the discovery that up to now your physical body has only been using the pattern of thinking that assumes separate parts are real: this or that in times and places.

The pattern of thinking of oneness gives priority to priorities: factors of times and places, separate parts, are absent.

Our physical body's patterns of thinking are like coatracks upon which it hangs its words like coats.

The unique thing about these coatracks is *whatever is its fundamental assumption about reality continues to unconsciously or self-consciously exist in its thinking in words when using it.*

If it is using the separate parts pattern of thinking, the *unconscious assumption* is the universe is separate parts.

If it is using the oneness pattern of thinking, the *self-consciously chosen assumption* is the universe is an indivisible whole.

Both are equally valuable!

The first allows us, the indivisible universe, to be self-conscious through our human being parts.

In its thinking, the second accurately represents as an inside belief the fact the universe operates as an indivisible whole.

Therefore, when being self-conscious your physical body wants to always be simultaneously using both patterns of thinking.

39

The separate parts pattern of thinking is operating as if all the parts are separate and, therefore, competing with all the other parts with the highest priority of each being its physical body's self-interest.

The oneness pattern of thinking is operating on the assumption all the parts are cooperating with each other for the health and maturation of the indivisible universe.

The fundamental pattern of thinking of the separate parts coatrack is *polarization*: this or that opposite separate part.

The fundamental pattern of thinking of the oneness coatrack is *prioritization*: including all the parts and giving priority to priorities.

As stated earlier, if the universe is an indivisible whole, there is no place to go from or to where your full physical body (the indivisible universe) is not already.

Different times and places, *the assumption of separate parts*, and *words* are mutually agreed upon illusion tools we invented through the use of our human parts to be simultaneously self-conscious in billions of locations.

They are valuable tools, and we want to continue to use them because we want to continue to be self-conscious.

However, your physical body now wants to give priority to the oneness coatrack, including all the parts and giving priority to priorities, because it accurately represents the universe operates as an indivisible whole.

There are no factors of times and places (separate parts) when thinking in priorities.
Priorities exist "at all times and in all places (in oneness)."
Giving priority to the priorities pattern of thinking is assuming oneness is a fact.

Your physical body is fully familiar with using the oneness pattern of thinking, the giving of priorities to priorities.
As described earlier, it does it whenever it is thinking about the inside of its skin, the one place where it currently assumes oneness. If it gets in an automobile accident and its leg needs to be amputated, it does not give priority to saving the leg and letting the physical body die.
It naturally gives priority to the whole body, second priority to one of its parts, and allows its leg to be amputated.
This is using the giving of priority to priorities pattern of thinking, the pattern of thinking that assumes oneness.
We earlier labeled this a "local oneness."

Our physical body does not need to learn the pattern of thinking of oneness!
It already knows it!
It uses it when thinking about the inside of its skin.
It now needs to learn to give the oneness pattern of thinking priority "at all times and in all places (in the fact of oneness)."

While simultaneously using both, our physical body now gives priority to the oneness pattern of thinking, giving priority to priorities, and second priority to the separate parts pattern of thinking, this or that in times and places.

Again, it wants to continue to use the latter because it allows your physical body to be self-conscious.
It also wants to simultaneously use the former because it accurately represents the fact the universe operates as an indivisible whole.

Our physical body soon discovers it is not possible to use both simultaneously if, *either unconsciously or self-consciously by choice,* it believes they both represent facts.
They are opposites.
That would be the equivalent of when leaving a driveway turning a Tesla right and left at the same time.
That is not possible, even for a Tesla!

This has your physical body eventually discover it can only do both fully and simultaneously, with no experience of conflict between them, when it knows the oneness pattern of thinking represents a fact and the separate parts pattern of thinking represents an illusion tool, a tool we invented through our human parts to have self-conscious parts.
It is a very valuable illusion tool.
But it is a mutually agreed upon illusion tool we invented so human beings could be our self-conscious parts.

It eventually discovers using both simultaneously is like when your physical body is playing Hamlet on a stage.
Everyone on stage, backstage, and in the audience knows you are real and Hamlet is an illusion.
However, for a couple of hours all are also in an agreement to make believe Hamlet is real.
Your physical body is now able to simultaneously be fully itself and Hamlet at the same time *with no experience of conflict.*

It accurately knows which one is real and which one is an illusion, as does everyone else on stage, backstage, and in the audience.

If your physical body began to think it was Hamlet, the director would stop the play and ask if there is a psychiatrist in the audience. The reason it can simultaneously be both *with no experience of conflict* is because it knows the *facts*: your physical body is real, and Hamlet is an illusion.

When your physical body knows oneness is a fact and the assumption of separate parts is a mutually agreed upon illusion tool we invented to have self-conscious parts, it can use both patterns of thinking fully and simultaneously with no experience of conflict.

This is only possible if your physical body always gives priority to the one that represents a fact, the oneness pattern of thinking, and second priority to the one it now knows is a mutually agreed upon illusion tool it invented to be self-conscious, the separate parts pattern of thinking.

Like being both yourself and Hamlet, it can then easily use both fully and simultaneously with no experience of conflict.

It now always gives priority to the oneness pattern of thinking, including all the parts and giving priority to priorities, and second priority to the separate parts pattern of thinking, choosing between this or that part in times and places.

Notice we, through your thinking, used the priority pattern of thinking to define the more mature self-definition in your thinking: "I am first the indivisible universe that will not die and secondly my physical body that will die, the only part of the universe where from the inside I have sole and complete control."

Notice also in your thinking we gave priority to being the oneness self-consciousness, the chooser, and second priority to being the separate part self-consciousness, the doer.

Now, anytime polarization between two good things emerge, your physical body will primarily see prioritization.

If all switch to using it, they can find agreement by putting the parts together to make a whole by identifying the most healthy and inclusive relationship for their time and situation.

Prioritization is including the third dimension of oneness.
When prioritization is the context of discussions, everyone's thinking automatically switches to putting the parts together to make a whole rather than choosing a side and fighting for that side.

43

Living a human life using only the this or that pattern of thinking is the equivalent of using your physical body's right hand to pluck out a melody on a piano.

It is only using the two-dimensions of assuming separate parts and notes and focused on their relationship with one another.

Adding a rhythm with the left hand, the same rhythm repeating while playing the melody with the right hand, is adding the *sensation of oneness*, the third dimension of human self-consciousness.

The rhythm is always the same just as oneness is always the same: oneness.
What has music experienced as beautiful is determined by which is given priority.

If the *priority* is oneness, the rhythm, while playing the melody, it is primarily experienced by the audience as the sensation of oneness. Fundamentally, that is what is experienced as beautiful.

The oneness pattern of thinking is being given priority.

If the priority in your thinking is the notes and their relationship with each other, it will be experienced as mechanical and not very beautiful: the focus will be on trying to get it right.

Priority is still being given to the two-dimensions of the notes and their relationship with one another, the this-or-that pattern of thinking.

Singing is the oldest ritual: all self-consciously moving as one.

Beauty in a human life is the same as the beauty in music.

It is the skill of knowing how to simultaneously use the three—the *assumption of separate parts, words,* and *oneness*—and give priority to the dimension that is real, oneness.

When your physical body is at full human maturity in the skill of human self-consciousness, it never ceases to give priority to the *three-dimensional sensation of oneness* while simultaneously using the illusory two dimensions of the assumption of separate parts and words to *self-consciously participate* in maturation.

This is another way to describe the activity of Eldering.

44

Your physical body can also eventually discover each moment it has been giving priority to priorities and not aware of it.

The oneness of nature cannot be escaped.

Therefore, the oneness pattern of thinking also cannot be escaped.

If your physical body uses mature free choice to study each moment, it will discover it always has a priority.

It then discovers it can be a self-conscious skill to freely choose its priority each moment.

Full maturity in the skill of mature free choice is your physical body self-consciously choosing its priority each moment.

It is the opposite of giving priority to reacting.

That is another way it unconsciously gives away its power to choose: it is allowing others to determine how it behaves.

At the Elder layer, regardless of what is occurring around it, your physical body freely choosing its priority each moment is full maturity in the use of mature free choice.

It is now also aware it was cooperation for maturation moving inside it that had it master the skill of each layer of maturity in the natural sequence.

Cooperation for maturation had our physical body's priority always be maturing into mastering the next layer of maturity when it had mastered the skill of the current layer it had been giving priority until it turned it into a habit.

Then the priority of its attention is free to discover and learn the smaller skill of the next layer.

It then becomes aware of the discomfort of knowing it is still not consistently living in natural contented joy.

It is that discomfort that has it know there must be the smaller skill of a next layer of maturity of this skill to learn.

Hopefully by now your physical body knows discomfort is a gift.

It is part of the natural process of cooperation for maturation always moving inside it that has that discomfort move it into searching for and discovering the smaller skill of each next layer when it is ready and able to learn it.

45

The Mature Elder layer is the next and last layer of maturity of the skill of human self-consciousness.

Like learning the smaller skills of riding a bicycle, at each layer your physical body can't master the smaller skills of the next layer until it has turned the smaller skills of the last layer not only into inside beliefs and skills but also into habits.

The skills of the lower layers need to be *habitually sustained* as the container for learning the skills of each next layer.

As stated earlier a couple of times, only then can it have its primary attention on discovering and mastering the smaller skills of the next layer.

Otherwise, and perhaps unconsciously, it will naturally still be giving priority to mastering the smaller skills of the last layer.

Therefore, to master the Mature Elder layer it is necessary to have changed the words in its thinking at the Elder layer into accurately representing as inside beliefs the four ways the indivisible universe operates at that layer: giving priority to mature free choice, having the accurate fundamental inside belief and self-definition and, while using both, giving priority to the oneness pattern of thinking and second priority to the separate parts pattern of thinking.

They must be in words that work for your physical body.

It is free to use whatever words it wants.

They are all equally illusions!

As mentioned earlier, there are over 6,000 human languages on Earth, and they are each mutually agreed upon illusion tools invented and sustained by a group of human beings.

The words it chooses can be in any human language, and they can within that language be whatever it likes.

*What is important is the words it chooses represent the **facts** of how the universe operates discovered at the Elder layer using mature free choice.*

Nearly all of humanity is overly ready to master the Elder layer. However, like all the lower layers, the last layer, the Mature Elder layer, cannot be easily understood and embraced as fact until the smaller skills of the Elder layer are mastered and turned into habits. Each layer of skills builds on the smaller skills of the layer before it.

46

Our first small skill at the Mature Elder layer is to primarily, self-consciously, and consistently enjoy the three-dimensional sensation of oneness.

It is the real sensation of being "a part of the universe" instead of the illusory sensation of being "a separate part."

These are your physical body's two possible to be known and experienced *fundamental sensations,* the sensations underneath its *relative sensations* of hearing, seeing, smelling, tasting, and touching.

The first one is the sensation it is experiencing when giving priority to three-dimensionality, the sensation of being "a part of the universe" or "a part of nature," whichever you prefer.

It is the same sensation we experienced as a Baby, the non-self-conscious sensation of being one with all that exists, only now your physical body also has the skill of human self-consciousness.

The second one, the sensation of being "a separate part," is the one your physical body is unconsciously, or self-consciously by choice, experiencing until it discovers it can be self-consciously aware of experiencing the first one, the sensation of being "a part of the universe."

Since learning a human language, up to this layer your physical body has been *unconsciously* giving priority to the fundamental sensation of only being its physical body, "a separate part."

It can now be introduced to the possibility the other fundamental sensation exists, that of being "a part of the universe."

Until it discovers the importance of maturing into giving priority to mature free choice, it will only exist as an idea in the two-dimensionality of human languages.

Only when it uses mature free choice to study its breathing does it discover the universe operates as an indivisible whole and, as a result, have the possibility of ***self-consciously experiencing*** the real fundamental sensation of three-dimensionality.

It is the *real fundamental sensation* of being "a part of the universe (nature)," rather than the *illusory fundamental sensation* of being "a separate part."

47

As mentioned earlier, there are three dimensions of the fully mature skill of human self-consciousness: *the assumption of separate parts, the use of words,* and *the oneness of nature.*

Your physical body now knows the first two are mutually agreed upon illusion tools it invented with others to enjoy the more mature pleasure of self-consciousness.

They are not real.

Only the third one, oneness, is real, a fact.

Also, now that it knows it is essential to give priority to the oneness pattern of thinking, including all the parts and giving priority to priorities, it knows it can self-consciously choose to give priority to oneness, *the sensation of oneness,* and second priority to the other two.

This it discovers is the sensation of three-dimensionality.

It is the *real fundamental sensation* of your physical body self-consciously experiencing itself as "a part of the universe."

The other possible fundamental sensation is what it has been unconsciously and sensually experiencing since learning words and up to when it discovers the sensation of oneness: the *fundamental illusory sensation* of being "a separate part."

It is not primarily *an inside belief in words* there is three-dimensionality.

It is also not primarily a *feeling.*

It is primarily a *sensation, the present experience of it.*

Once it uses mature free choice to become aware of the sensation of being "a part of the universe," the significant greater joy of experiencing it will reveal it is a fact.

Your physical body will then never be able to fool itself into thinking it does not know it is "a part of the three-dimensional universe."

It will be joyfully stuck mastering this important first of four smaller skills at the Mature Elder layer of maturity: giving priority in thinking to the fundamental sensation of three-dimensionality, the able to be self-consciously known sensation of oneness.

It is the sensual experience of being "a part of the indivisible universe," **living in the reality of self-conscious three-dimensionality.**

48

If your physical body looks around the room where it is right now, it will notice it can become aware it is a three-dimensional experience.

Although your physical body does not normally turn its attention to it, it can become aware of three-dimensionality.
It is similar to what we experience when watching a three-dimensional movie.

When in the habit of giving priority to one of the lowest five layers, it is assuming two-dimensionality: the assumption of separate parts and words are the only two dimensions of the skill of human self-consciousness present in its thinking.
When walking through a room, it thinks it is primarily seeing the lamp and the chair.
It is seeing them, but it is not *primarily* seeing them.
It is primarily seeing *the words* "lamp" and "chair," unconsciously seeing them as separate parts like words.

When it is changing the lightbulb in the lamp, it is then primarily experiencing it as a three-dimensional object.
It needs to do so to change the lightbulb.
The rest of the time it is not aware of it, but it is primarily experiencing the lamp as the word "lamp."
In its thinking, it is primarily relating with words.

The practical way to include the third dimension of oneness is to experience the fundamental sensation of three-dimensionality as the context of everything your physical body experiences.

It discovers that is acknowledging the presence of oneness, the third dimension of human self-consciousness that is the only one that is real, and it then naturally gives it priority.
This has it experience the *sensation* of being "a part in the room" rather than being "a separate part."

This sensation of three-dimensionality is the self-consciously known sensation of being "a part in the room" rather than "a separate part":
the self-consciously known sensation of oneness

49

The best way to become aware your physical body can self-consciously experience the *sensation of three-dimensionality* is to walk around the house and become aware it is "a part of what it is experiencing."

Then become aware of the sensation of it: the sensation of being connected to all around it and a part of everything.

It will become aware of this as a sensation, *the present experience* of being "a part of it" rather than "a separate part."

The latter is the illusory fundamental sensation of not being connected to and a part of anything outside your physical body.

When it becomes self-consciously aware of the difference between these two possible fundamental sensations, it will immediately know which one is more enjoyable.

Once it is aware in present experience of the difference between them, like knowing rocks are hard and fire is hot, it will never be able to fool itself into thinking it does not know the difference between them.

Your physical body will then be stuck self-consciously living in the reality of the *three-dimensional sensation of self-conscious oneness.*

Wherever your physical body is, we would like to suggest, after reading this page, you get up and spend a few minutes walking around and simply be self-consciously aware of the fact it is "a part of all you are experiencing," not "a separate part."

That is the sensation of self-conscious oneness.

It is being simultaneously aware of all three dimensions of human self-consciousness—the assumption of separate parts, words, and oneness—and by nature and now by choice giving priority to the one that is real, oneness, and *simultaneously* using the other two.

This is the three-dimensional sensation of self-conscious oneness.

Being a self-conscious part of three-dimensional reality is the first of the four skills of choosing to operate at the highest layer of maturity of this skill, the Mature Elder layer.

Do not let this remain only as words here and in your thinking, in two-dimensionality; begin living in reality, in self-conscious 3D.

Do get your physical body up and for some time walk it around into different locations while simply being self-consciously (by choice) aware of the **sensation** it is "a part of all it is experiencing."

Please do that now and decide if it is more enjoyable.

~ **50** ~

It is important to note your physical body can't be rid of a pattern of behavior by choosing to get rid of it.

That is focusing on it that reinforces it.

It must know the pattern of behavior to replace it and instead choose to focus on it, easy to do when it knows it is more enjoyable. When it finds itself habitually doing the less mature behavior, *if it has discovered the more mature behavior using mature free choice,* when it becomes aware of its regression it will naturally, effortlessly, freely, and immediately, and without the need of effort, force, or discipline, choose the more mature behavior.

This is allowing the natural fundamental process of maturation operating in its thinking to be maturing it, to do the work.

When it discovers the joy of self-consciously experiencing each moment within the context of the three-dimensional sensation of oneness, it quickly learns to choose it any time any uncomfortable, "not good enough," fears, wants, and desires emerge in its thinking. It is the antidote to all of them.

*This choice instantly returns it to **contented joy** as the context of everything that is occurring because it is honoring the **fact** the universe operates as an indivisible whole.*

The joy of this sensation, the self-consciously known three-dimensional sensation of oneness, is what cooperation for maturation uses to mature it into becoming a habit.

Like you experienced the sensation of a local oneness inside your skin, your physical body is now experiencing the room as another sensation of a local oneness.

However, it now knows there is only one oneness.

Giving priority to self-consciously experiencing everything within the three-dimensional sensation of oneness is the **direct self-conscious experience of the oneness of the universe as a sensation.**

It now knows the sensation of oneness anywhere is the sensation of oneness everywhere.

There is only one able to be self-consciously known sensation of oneness, the sensation of three-dimensionality.

51

The self-consciously known three-dimensional sensation of one-ness can only be experienced in the now.
Only the now is real.

The past and future only exist in the mutually agreed upon illusion tools of words.
Our human physical body eventually discovers there are two nows, the Oneness Now and the Relative Now.

The Oneness Now is all the past, present, and future as one sensation, the self-consciously known three-dimensional sensation of oneness.
The Relative Now is the sensation of the now between the past and future, the illusory sensation of being a separate part.

Like the discovery of all important facts using mature free choice, maturation into giving priority to the Oneness Now will happen naturally, effortlessly, freely, and permanently.
It will happen the same way knowing rocks are hard and fire is hot became accurate inside beliefs in its thinking, skills to honor those facts, and habits no longer in need of its primary attention.
And its maturation into giving priority to the Oneness Now, the fundamental sensation of three-dimensionality, will happen without the need of effort, force, or discipline.
Like its mastery in the natural sequence of the smaller skills of the lower six layers of human maturation, it will be the result of the natural process of cooperation for maturation always moving inside everything, including your physical body's thinking.

The Oneness Now is real.
The Relative Now is not real, but, like the assumption of separate parts, it is a valuable mutually agreed upon illusion tool that allows us to be self-conscious parts of the indivisible universe, to analyze the past, develop a plan for the future, and consistently execute it in both the Oneness and Relative Nows, alone or with others.

Only the Oneness Now is real.
Everything else only exists in the mutually agreed upon illusion tools of words.

52

Your physical body's layer of maturity determines its relationship skills with itself and others.

Parental training determines the habits until the Teen layer.

Self-eldering determines them from that layer forward.

At full maturity, relative sensations are known to occur; they are not experienced as bad (immature) or good (mature); they are just experienced (mature Baby layer).

Relative feelings also occur; they can be mature or immature.

What determines them is your physical body's layer of maturity.

At full maturity at the highest layer its primary feelings are natural confidence, contented joy, and compassion.

It has matured out of strongly experiencing immature feelings of some derivative of mad and scared (mature Toddler layer).

Wants can also be mature or immature.

At full maturity your priority is cooperation with the other parts for the maturation of the indivisible universe, self-conscious participation in the fundamental process in nature (mature Child layer).

At full maturity individual free choice also gives this priority (mature Teen layer).

As you mature your physical body's most important beliefs become based on facts using mature free choice (inside beliefs).

Being right is no longer good; being wrong is no longer bad.

With your physical body and that of others, you can talk about things in search of agreement on facts rather than only make decisions.

You can also gather more facts to form deeper held agreements (mature Adult layer).

You can also agree on the words, your self-definition, and the relationship of the two possible patterns of thinking you will use with yourself and others to represent those facts (mature Elder layer).

Your physical body can only consistently enjoy the self-consciously known sensation of oneness and Eldering to the degree it has mastered the skills of the lower layers (mature Mature Elder layer).

Your physical body's layer of maturity in the skill of human self-consciousness determines how it experiences everything.

~ **53** ~

Choosing three-dimensionality, the fundamental sensation of being "a part of the universe," as the context of all your human physical body experiences is giving priority to the third dimension of oneness as a *sensation, your physical body's most direct relationship with the universe* (the Baby layer).

The next level of direct relationship with the universe is the level of *feelings* (Toddler layer).
When self-consciously aware of three-dimensionality, your physical body discovers it is experiencing the *three fundamental feelings* that are possible to experience: natural confidence, contented joy, and compassion.
They are discovered to be underneath and now more important for it to know and self-consciously experience than its relative feelings of some derivative of mad, glad, sad, and scared.
The fundamental feelings have been there all along and it has often self-consciously experienced them.
It now knows them as *always present*; and, at the feeling layer, it uses mature free choice to give them priority over its relative feelings.

The next layer of direct relationship with the universe is the use of the *assumption of separate parts* and *words* that allow it to be self-conscious (Child layer).

The next layer of direct relationship with the universe is *exercising individual free choice* (Teen layer).

After usually many changes in its choices, it can eventually have *its outside belief replaced with the inside belief the universe operates as an indivisible whole* (Adult layer).

The next layer is using mature free choice to study its breathing to discover this is the most fundamental fact of how the universe operates and represent it as an inside belief.

This is primarily being a personal scientist (Elder layer).

It is at the last layer it discovers it is only us, the indivisible universe, the only thing that is real (Mature Elder layer).

54

Your physical body can now see the importance of always giving priority to the oneness pattern of thinking coatrack, including all the parts and giving priority to priorities.

This allows it to know the smaller skills of the layers of maturity of the skill of human self-consciousness now exist in its thinking as priorities in an order of importance that is the exact order in which it learned them.

Now its highest priority is the self-consciously known three-dimensional sensation of oneness.
It is the *real fundamental sensation* possible for it to know by using mature free choice to discover the fact the universe operates as an indivisible whole.
The *illusory fundamental sensation* of being a separate part can also be experienced.
It did, indeed, experience it as real up to its discovery of the self-consciously known three-dimensional sensation of oneness.
However, the sensation of being a separate part was based on an illusion; it was the equivalent of feeling frightened by a scene in a movie.
The sensation is real; our physical body is experiencing it.
But it is the result of an illusion, a movie.

It now knows the **natural contented joy** *of experiencing everything occurring within the fundamental oneness sensation of three-dimensionality—experiencing the sensation of being "a part of everything;" this confirms that sensation is the result of a fact, the fact the universe operates as an indivisible whole.*

It will then quickly become a habit to always be aware of it as the context of everything else it experiences.
As mentioned earlier, if old immature habits of behavior it doesn't like emerge, it also knows it can immediately return to *self-consciously choosing* to experience the three-dimensional sensation of oneness, being "a part of everything," as the context of everything it is experiencing.
It will be instantly recognized as far more enjoyable.

55

What we, the indivisible universe, are always doing is maturing in and through everything, including each human being's thinking. *One of the ways we do this is by downloading into words in your thinking information that is valuable for you to know.*

Before the last two layers, your thinking usually began in words, processed in words, and reached conclusions in words.

Your physical body was only using two of the three dimensions: the assumption of separate parts and words.

It was not aware that as part of our cooperation for maturation process we are always downloading important information *directly into your thinking in words.*

Has your physical body ever misplaced your cell phone and then, while taking a shower, have the words come into your thinking of where you left it?

That is not only memory operating inside your physical body.

That is also us directly providing information that is valuable to you: *it is from your direct relationship with us.*

Terry's thinking, the human being I am using to write this book, has now learned to always be listening for the information we are always downloading into words in his physical body's thinking.

He is aware that during the day he is so in the world of words it is not easy to do, to notice these direct downloads in words.

However, he is naturally developing a habit of being aware of it because its information is always experienced as valuable.

Early each morning, when it is still dark outside, he gets in his hot tub on the deck and listens.

To do so, he begins with affirming "I am only the indivisible universe: it is doing my breathing."

Then he asks, "What is the truth here? What is the best for the common good of all?"

Then he just listens—he patiently listens.

The important new insights he needs to know come into his thinking in words from us and continually come into it.

Give this form of meditation a try.

If your physical body does not learn the importance of listening to us, it won't become good at hearing us.

We, the indivisible universe, is always very practical, and we always have only one agenda: cooperation for maturation.

56

Here is the second of the four smaller skills your physical body can learn at the Mature Elder layer.

It only discovers it when it has mastered as a skill and habit the full skill of human self-consciousness, self-consciously giving priority to the three-dimensional sensation of oneness—the first of the four smaller skills at this layer.

Then it can discover the fact it is *only* us, the indivisible universe.

It now knows its physical body does not exist as a separate part.

Like all perceptions of parts as separate, it is an illusion.

From the inside it is true it only has sole and complete control over its physical body, but that does not have it exist separate from everything else.

Through your physical body, we are being self-conscious at your location.

That means your physical body is also a tool we use and you can know we are using it as a tool when you experience the natural contented joy of self-consciously participating in cooperation for maturation, our fundamental process.

In its thinking, it now experiences its physical body not only as a part of the indivisible universe but also as an illusory tool it can use for self-conscious participation in maturation.

It is a mutually agreed upon illusion tool we also invented when we invented the assumption of separate parts and words.

It is a different part with different abilities, but it is not a separate part.

It now does not take what other people say or do personally.

This is also what has it accept full responsibility for what it does with this tool.

This is also what has it naturally, effortlessly, freely, and permanently, without the need of effort, force, or discipline, accept people and situations as they are and only have its attention each moment on how it can be loving, on Eldering.

In the words of the East, this is the natural source of non-atTFACh-ment, equanimity.

In the words of the West, this is the natural source of happiness.

In your thinking, your physical body now knows the fact it is *only* the indivisible universe, *the only thing that is real.*
Seeing your physical body as separate is now correctly seen as one of the tools being used by us, just like the assumption of separate parts and words are valuable illusion tools we use.
There are not separate parts.
Your perception of the parts as different is accurate.
Any perception of them as separate from one another is an illusion, accurately seen as a tool used by us for you to master the *skill* of human self-consciousness.
Only the indivisible universe is real.

Your physical body now knows the perception of it in thinking using words as a physical body is seeing it as a separate part.
You now only perceive it as an inseparable part of us and, therefore, as only us, the indivisible universe.
And any perception of it as your physical body is now seeing it as a tool.
It also knows it needed to operate on the assumption the universe is separate parts while mastering the early layers of maturity of the skill of human self-consciousness.

There was no other way to have mastered them.

Only then was it possible for its physical body to use mature free choice to discover and master the last two layers.

It now knows it has the full mature skill of human self-consciousness and that is not the end goal of its life.
We had a purpose for you mastering it.
It was so we could have a self-consciously skilled human being in your location to cooperate with the other parts for our continuous maturation.

We, the indivisible universe, is doing everyone's breathing and each human being is self-consciously participating in our cooperation for maturation at its location.
This is now accurately known as a fact.
This is now accurately known as real.

58

Once you have mastered the smaller skills of experiencing every-thing occurring in three-dimensionality, and knowing you are only the indivisible universe, you are ready to master the next smaller skill: *the direct choice of the self-consciously known sensation of oneness.*

The way Terry has accomplished this is by repeating the words, "There is no Terry Mollner" and noticing the sensation left.
He does not focus on the words; he focuses on the sensation that emerges when he knows those words state a fact.
It is the self-conscious three-dimensional sensation of oneness.
It is the sensation of *who he really is*, the indivisible universe.

He discovered he was not able to directly know it, experience it, and choose it because he was still, *at a deep level of unconsciousness,* identifying himself as only his physical body part of himself. Only when he self-consciously chose to eliminate the existence of Terry Mollner was he able to directly know, experience, and choose the sensation of oneness the same way he knows, experiences, and chooses the sensation rocks are hard and fire is hot: immediately and habitually.
By default, it is what is left in self-consciousness: *the direct self-conscious experience of the three-dimensional sensation of oneness.*

Terry uses those words to fully eliminate the assumption of the ex-istence of Terry Mollner as only his physical body within his skin. He sometimes uses the words, "The universe is an indivisible whole and I am it."
It makes no difference what words he or you use as long as they work to eliminate the existence of you as only your physical body within your skin part of you.
Find the words that work for you.
When your chosen words succeed, you are left only with a sensation, the self-consciously known 3D sensation of oneness.

Before turning to the next page, see if you can discover this **self-conscious awareness of the sensation of oneness** by repeating this fact to allow it to emerge, "There is no (add your name)."

∼ 59 ∽

Your physical body is fully aware of the sensation of being alive instead of being dead: self-conscious aliveness.
That sensation of being alive is the sensation of oneness.
Until you discover the indivisible universe is the only thing that is real, you think it is the sensation of your physical body being alive. It then knows it is the sensation of you, the indivisible universe, being one of its self-conscious parts your physical body controls.
Up until then you have been giving it the wrong name.
That is the *deepest unconscious way (without choice)* you still have been identifying yourself as only your physical body.

As you now know, when being self-conscious words are always between you and what you are thinking, seeing, or doing.
You can now rename the sensation of being alive its accurate name and know the importance of doing so.
The indivisible universe is the only thing that is real.
Therefore, the accurate name for the sensation of being alive is the sensation of oneness.

It is not something new you need to learn!
You already know it!
You just need to rename it!
The sensation of being alive is the sensation of oneness!

You need to rename it the accurate name so your words will no longer stop you from knowing and enjoying the experience of knowing the sensation of being alive is the sensation of oneness.

As you live into using mature free choice to know the fact the universe operates as an indivisible whole and naming the sensation of being alive the sensation of oneness, what confirms it is a fact is you discover *the more enjoyable feelings* of natural confidence, contented joy, and compassion emerge inside your physical body and take priority over your relative feelings of some derivatives of mad, glad, sad, and scared.

This confirms for you the sensation of being alive is the sensation of oneness.
This is the last smaller skill you need to learn as a Mature Elder.

60

After reading this page, choose the following experience.
Using mature free choice, you now know the universe operates as an indivisible whole.
That means it is the only thing that is real.
Everything else is within the illusion there are separate parts.
Self-consciousness operates on the assumption there are separate parts when there aren't separate parts.
This valuable mutually agreed upon illusion tool we invented is what allows your physical body to be self-conscious.
You are not only your physical body or that tool.
You are only the indivisible universe.
There are not two things: you and oneness.
There is only oneness.

At the deepest unconscious level, you are probably still acting as if it is your physical body that is alive.
That is the deepest place of unconsciously assuming your physical body is a separate part.

You correct this by choosing what you now know is a fact: your sensation of being alive is the three-dimensional sensation of oneness. Then noticing you like how this changes your experience.

After reading this page, use the following words to focus your attention not on those words but on **the experience** of knowing this is a fact: **"my sensation of being alive is the three-dimensional sensation of oneness, the only thing that is real."**

We suggest you keep your eyes open so you can experience it in relationship to everything around you.
Just hang out with this fact after reading this page and choose it as often as you like in future days **until you consistently know the choice of the experience of this fact as a skill.**

Allow me to repeat the above paragraph to guide you:
After reading this page, use the following words to focus your attention not on those words but on **the experience** of knowing this is a fact: **"my sensation of being alive is the three-dimensional sensation of oneness, the only thing that is real."**

61

After reading the last page, our guess is when you chose to *experience* the sensation of being alive as the self-consciously known three dimensional sensation of oneness you liked what you experienced. At the deepest conditioned place inside you, your physical body is no longer dealing with a competitive relationship with everything else.

It is fully released from that activity.

Also, there is nothing left you must do.

There are no separate parts you must deal with.

You probably labeled it "peacefulness" or a similar word.

This is *mature freedom*: there is nothing you must do, and you are free to do whatever you like.

Most important, there is not the experience of the existence of a second thing with which we need to relate.

That is why it is labeled by us "mature freedom."

What do you now do?

You will only be interested in doing one thing: Eldering.

Each moment, you will only be interested in giving priority to whatever you judge to be the best thing you can do as a self-conscious participant in cooperation for maturation with what you now know are your other parts, the fundamental process of nature.

Nothing is more enjoyable than self-conscious Eldering.

Thus, you will now not be able to stop yourself from doing it.

When Eldering, you are *self-consciously moving as one with all* and that is why our fundamental process of maturation had you mature into full maturity in the skill of human self-consciousness.

Our fundamental process of maturation is to have all human beings primarily Eldering before the end of their teenage years.

Since maturation cannot be escaped or stopped, this is inevitable.

Hopefully you are one of the human beings who has now achieved this highest layer of maturity in the skill of human self-consciousness.

If so, wherever you are, let yourself do the happy dance!

As was noted a couple of times earlier, the one place your physical body currently assumes oneness is inside its skin.

It can imagine it is only its arm, leg, liver, or heart because it can imagine anything.

But it cannot *know* it is only one of them.

It *already knows the fact* it is its entire physical body.

In the same way, when it knows the universe operates as an indivisible whole, it also *cannot know it is only its physical body.*

It *now knows the fact* it is only the indivisible universe, the only thing that is real.

And as it knows the parts within its physical body are different but not separate, it now knows the parts within its total physical body, the indivisible universe, are also different but not separate.

This is what has it no longer take anything personally.
It is no longer only its physical body within its skin that will die.
It is now only the indivisible universe that will not die.

Knowing this is a *fact* by using mature free choice to confirm it is a fact *and also habitually and immediately giving priority to the sensation of oneness* has your physical body consistently experience it. It is this that has it know the fundamental feelings of natural confidence, contented joy, and compassion and has it now always give them priority over its relative feelings of some derivative of mad, glad, sad, and scared.

It is this that has its priority in its actions each moment be Eldering.

It is this that each moment has it experience its life as meaningful.

It now knows what to give priority in its actions each moment: Eldering.

We, the universe, is going somewhere.

Metaphorically, not somewhere out and about but somewhere up.

We are at all times and in all places (in oneness) maturing.

Through your physical body you now know you are only us; you are enjoying the sensation of oneness; you are Eldering; and you are self-consciously participating at your location in the fundamental process in us: cooperation for maturation.

Growing up you thought you were only your physical body.

You were unaware you were using the illusions of the assumption of separate parts and words to master this skill.

~ 63 ~

In thinking and action, your physical body now knows its highest priority is enjoying the three-dimensional sensation of oneness, *the sensation of being oneness,* and second priority is Eldering.
How to live your life meaningfully is now obvious.

It is using the oneness pattern of thinking to at all times and in all places (in oneness) have these two priorities in this order.
This is what allows it to enjoy the fundamental feelings of *natural confidence* (using mature free choice to discover oneness is a fact), *contented joy* (always self-consciously experiencing everything within the three-dimensional sensation of oneness), and *compassion* (its loving relationship with the other parts as parts of itself).
When operating at full maturity at the Mature Elder layer, this knowledge becomes inside beliefs in its thinking, skills, and habits. Then each moment its attention is free to focus on identifying what it determines is its best action, large or small, of self-conscious participation in our fundamental process—cooperation with the other parts for the health and maturation of us, Eldering.

Only these priorities in its thinking and actions sustain within its physical body the fundamental feelings of natural confidence, contented joy, and compassion.
Its doer self-consciousness is always honoring that cooperation for maturation is the fundamental process in us, always the choice of its chooser self-consciousness.

Nothing is more enjoyable than the knowledge and sensation it is only us that is real.
Your physical body has mastered the full skill of human self-consciousness that has it know how to choose the enjoyable 3D sensation of oneness as the accurate sensation of being alive.
And it knows, each moment, Eldering is the only priority *in its thinking and actions* that sustains this enjoyable sensation of oneness in its physical body because only Eldering is *self-conscious participation* in cooperation for maturation, the fundamental process in nature.

64

When mastering the smaller skills of the first five layers of the skill of human self-consciousness, your physical body, *by necessity*, assumed it is a part separate from us.

Also, at full maturity in this skill, it concluded it is a part of us, the indivisible universe, and gives priority to being us and second priority to being its part of us, uses prioritization.

But, like all it perceives in its thinking in words, *behaviorally those are both experienced as separate parts.*

Everything your physical body perceives in its thinking is separate parts, even the indivisible universe, *because they all exist within the assumption of separate parts using words.*

Nothing in your thinking in words can be other than a separate part.

Using self-consciousness, *your physical body can only* **know** *it is only the indivisible universe and* **it can only know it with natural confidence** *when it uses mature free choice to study its breathing.*

When full maturity in the skill of human self-consciousness is achieved, it is the direct experience **by choice** to give priority to the three-dimensional sensation of oneness that has it know we are writing this through Terry's physical body tool.

There is not a second thing!

Everything your physical body perceives in its thinking is not only a different part of the indivisible universe but also only the indivisible universe because the different parts are not separate from one another *except in the mutually agreed upon illusions of words in self-conscious thinking.*

Everything your physical body perceives is inside its one physical body, the indivisible universe.

The parts are different but, like you perceive the parts within your skin, they are not separate from one another.

In your thinking, your physical body now gives priority to the priority of your total physical body, the indivisible universe.

But that is not only thinking in words!

It now also knows the fact it is only the indivisible universe.

Every part it perceives in its thinking will "die," change form.

The indivisible universe is the only thing that is real and will not die.

Mature, yes; die, no.

Just as it takes no time to go from being your physical body's right hand to being its left hand because it *already knows* it is both of them and all of its physical body in between them, it *now knows* it takes no time to go from being any perceived different part of the universe to another.

It *now knows* it is both and all the physical parts in between.

And just as it knows only in its perception in thinking can its right hand be both different and separate from its left hand, it *now knows it experiences them as two different but not separate parts of one whole, its physical body*.

At full maturity in the skill of human self-consciousness it now also knows it experiences every different part of the universe the exact same way it experiences all the different parts within its skin, as different but not as separate parts.

The indivisible universe is the only thing that is real.

The parts are different, but they are not separate.

*As a personal scientist using mature free choice to study its breathing, your physical body now knows these are what are labeled **facts**.*

It also knows the mutually agreed upon illusion tools the human parts invented, the assumption of separate parts and words, were invented to be used as tools that allow us, the indivisible universe, to be at the same time self-conscious in billions of locations.

This was a maturation of us and there will continue to be maturations of us.

Cooperation for maturation cannot be escaped or stopped.

It is your physical body's fully mature skill of human self-consciousness that allows it to **know these facts** and the rest of its life primarily enjoy Eldering in its thinking and actions.

For our self-conscious parts, the most important facts used in their thinking are the ones identified using mature free choice.

Once discovered using it, it can't ever fool itself into thinking it does not know them.

They then naturally, effortlessly, and freely become facts you know are accurate, then skills, and then habits no longer in need of your primary attention.

When many of our human beings achieve full maturity in the skill of human self-consciousness, it will naturally mature everything else in their lives.
When doing it with others, it will be living together within the fact they are only the indivisible universe.
They will mutually enjoy the three-dimensional sensation of oneness as the container of the illusions of two-dimensionality that allows them to be self-conscious parts of the indivisible universe.

Their physical bodies will also know they have achieved full maturity in the skill of human self-consciousness because they now know there could not be a higher layer of that skill.
They know it is not possible to primarily define "self" as anything larger than us, the indivisible universe.

Therefore, each moment their physical bodies are now free to have their attention on Eldering.

The direct habitual experience of the sensation of oneness is not an accomplished static state in which they wallow.
It is a dynamic state, always in motion, and only the priority of Eldering in their thinking and actions sustains the sensation of oneness inside their physical bodies and the fundamental feelings of natural confidence, contented joy, and compassion.

It is also not possible to separate anything from everything else.
Now their priority each moment is to use their physical body tools to be active self-conscious participants in the maturation of the rest of who we are, the indivisible universe.

This is now their total physical bodies' mature self-interest.

And there is no need of effort, force, or discipline.
In all they do, the natural process of cooperation for maturation occurring within everything will have Eldering naturally, effortlessly, freely, and consistently happen.

67

You are still your physical body!

From the inside you still have sole and complete control of it.

You still have relative sensations and feelings; you still use the words of a human language; you are still self-conscious.

You still exercise individual free choice and mature free choice.

You still have outside and inside beliefs.

There is just one difference: you now have the fully mature skill of human self-consciousness.

From using mature free choice, you now know the universe operates as an indivisible whole and you are an indivisible-from-it-part-of-it.

Therefore, you are only it, the only thing that is real.

You directly experience that fact as the self-consciously known three-dimensional sensation of oneness.

Genuine humility is never acting as if your physical body is separate from the indivisible universe.

The difference from operating at the lower six layers is you now know there are not separate parts.

That is the only difference, and it changes your relationship with everything else.

Either the universe operates as one thing or as separate parts.
There is not a third option.
You needed to operate on the illusion it is separate parts to discover self-consciousness, learn words, and mature in self-consciousness.
Only when that skill is mastered can you use mature free choice to discover the fact the universe operates as an indivisible whole.

The reason we had you operate on the assumption it is separate parts was to have us have the skill of self-consciousness at the location of your physical body and all human physical bodies.

We wanted this maturation into the skill of human self-consciousness to occur so we could continue our fundamental process of cooperation for maturation self-consciously.

That is what will now be occurring: self-conscious cooperation for maturation.

Each day into the future there will be more personal scientists who have achieved full maturity in the skill of human self-consciousness.

68

This experience of the self-consciously known three-dimensional sensation of oneness reminded Terry of in 1979 when, for three months, he traveled the trains in India visiting people still alive who had worked closely with Mahatma Gandhi.

When he revealed that was what he was doing when in conversations with people on the trains, he almost always immediately got a response something like this, "Forget about Gandhi! He was not a normal human being!"

What they were saying is he was not operating at one of the five lower layers of human maturation where the highest priority is still the self-interest of our human physical body as if a separate part.

It is important to know this will often be the response to one genuinely operating at the Mature Elder layer of maturity, giving priority to the self-consciously known three-dimensional sensation of oneness.

You will learn to not be surprised by this response or let it cause you to worry you are doing something wrong.

It is the normal response of someone operating at the fifth or lower layer *as if it is the highest layer*.

You will immediately double-check to make sure you are giving priority to the self-consciously known three-dimensional sensation of oneness and that your thoughts and actions are on Eldering.

Then you will relate lovingly with the other or others as parts of yourself.

You will know they are operating at a lower layer of human maturation as if it is the highest layer; and, if they knew of the next higher layer, they would want to master it.

About this they do not have choice.

That is the natural process of maturation always moving inside all of us.

If you identify a way you could be helpful, and they would appreciate it, you will also not be able to stop yourself from doing it.

Eldering is now what you naturally do.

69

You are now primarily a Maturation Movement activist.

A "good movement" is the word human beings have given to identifying a fact everyone has not fully embraced.
It is an on-going education program to assist all to come to know and fully embrace that fact.

You now know cooperation for maturation, not competition, is the fundamental process in nature.
However, everyone has not matured to know this fact.
The Maturation Movement is the on-going educational program to assist all to come to know this fact, both through conversations, study groups, and educational entertainment, and through building organizations based on it.

The Civil Rights-Black Lives Matter Movement is an example of a good movement to assist people to know the fact all people with colored skin are equally human beings and have equal rights with people with white skin.
The Woman's Movement is an example of a good movement to assist people to know the fact all women are equally human beings and have equal rights with male human beings.

All human beings who have achieved full maturity in the skill of human self-consciousness will be unable to stop themselves from being active participants in the Maturation Movement.
Playing a quiet or not so quiet role in the maturation of all and their organizations is now their mature self-interest.
Nothing can stop them from giving priority in their thinking and actions to Eldering.

It is the only priority in their thinking and actions that sustains the joy of the three-dimensional sensation of oneness and fundamental feelings of natural confidence, contented joy, and compassion.

This will also mature all their relationships with others.
Here are some examples of this.

In romance, when seeking a lover what will be most important is his or her physical body has also achieved full maturity in the skill of human self-consciousness.

Only a love relationship operating at this layer of maturity will last forever, they will know it will last forever, and it will be enjoyable each moment.

They will know it primarily exists in the Oneness Now.

*They will **mutually know** they are both living within the fact they are only the indivisible universe and the enjoyment of the self-consciously known three-dimensionality of the sensation of oneness.*

This will have them always give priority *in their thinking and actions* to cooperation with all the other parts for the health and maturation not only of their children but also of the rest of the indivisible universe, the activity of Eldering.

They will then join with others who have achieved this into communities of friends, a re-villaging of their lives, to also participate as communities in the cooperation for maturation process of nature.

When Terry's physical body was 72 years old, he met Lucy, who was 70, and they both had that experience of love at first sight.

He recognized it as the sensation of oneness he wanted to always have with a woman and invited her to join him in giving it priority each moment to allow it to teach them how to know it naturally and effortlessly with each other as a skill they could choose.

For Terry, it took three years and several mistakes before it revealed to him there is only one oneness, and he is only it.

Each time when he thought he had learned what it wanted to teach him, he discovered he was wrong and returned to giving priority to the experience of love at first sight they had experienced.

It eventually taught him the four smaller skills at the Mature Elder layer.

Now, their physical bodies, each in its own way, enjoy consistently living with each other in the fact the sensation of being alive is the sensation of oneness, self-consciously known 3D.

They mistakenly thought it was only between the two of them.

There is only one oneness.

As parents, our physical bodies will know our most important responsibility is to Elder our children to full maturity in the skill of human self-consciousness before they leave home and marry.

This will include having them be consistently aware, beginning at an early age, it is a skill they will be learning, there are smaller skills that result in the full skill, and they can only learn them in the natural progression.

Also, the smaller skills of some layers can only be learned when their physical bodies are able to learn them.
Their physical bodies and brains need to be sufficiently developed.

Thus, as parents, we need to learn the skill of assisting each child to learn each smaller skill at each layer when each is ready and able to learn it.
We then assist them to become aware they have learned each layer and eventually they will surely give them names they have chosen.
They will then know the skill of human self-consciousness is a skill, there are smaller skills to learn at each layer of learning it, and there are the smaller skills at the highest layer.
They will then not be content until they have self-eldered themselves to full maturity in this most important skill for them to learn.
Since only each can Elder themselves up the last three layers of maturity of this skill, having them learn of the existence of the layers of maturity by name when they are growing up is essential to set them on this course.

*When they have mastered the smaller skills of a layer, as parents **we need to change the way we relate with them to honor they have achieved it.***
This is an important Eldering skill to master when Eldering our children.

At the early teen years, as parents it is especially important to honor our children's physical bodies have mentally matured to have the ability and right to exercise individual free choice.

The days of them obeying us to survive are over.

It is essential our physical bodies recognize this maturation and, when reaching agreements with them, now use a consensus process.

Also, from this point forward they have full responsibility for self-eldering their physical bodies up the remaining layers to achieve full maturity in this skill.

Unlike the first four layers where we taught them the smaller skills, now no one else has the power to make sure they learn the smaller skills of the last three layers.

The remaining layers of maturity are a self-eldering job.

Their physical bodies now must use their skill of exercising individual free choice, and then mature free choice, to discover and master the smaller skills of the last three layers.

We can be helpful, particularly by assisting them to discover the importance of maturing into using mature free choice.

It will be necessary for them to learn it to master the last two layers.

If we have done a good job of having them be aware they were learning the smaller skills of each layer by name during their childhood, they will be fully aware there are layers of maturity of this skill.

This will have the natural process of maturation moving inside them have them seek to master the smaller skills of the last few layers, using whatever words they choose to name them.

If our Eldering is wise, they can even skip the Adult layer of giving their power to an outside belief in words and move from the Teen layer into using mature free choice to master the Elder layer.

This Eldering of our children is an art as much as a skill.

And nothing is experienced as more fulfilling than Eldering our children to full maturity in the skill of human self-consciousness before they leave home: it is the direct enjoyment of the sensation of oneness and Eldering.

73

If our human physical bodies have done a good job of Eldering their children up the first four layers, and mutual respect is strong, as parents you will know the importance of not using force, unless necessary to save them from danger, and be fully available to Elder them into the discovery and mastery of the smaller skills of the last two layers that, it is important to note, must primarily be a self-eldering process by them.
It is an inside job.

Finally, if the school they attend is not giving priority to Eldering them up the mastery of this most important skill to learn, you will work with other parents to create a complimentary educational program that focuses on the mastery of this skill and all the many smaller skills as an extension of it, for instance relationship, economic, finance, democratic, and other life skills.

As stated earlier, it is possible for our children to achieve full maturity in the skill of human self-consciousness before they leave home, join with another in marriage, and join with others in community and work.

Mature parenting can have this happen.
Then, if our children marry, they will more probably marry people who have also achieved full maturity in this skill.
They will then together enjoy giving priority in their thinking and actions to Eldering the rest of their lives, not only of their children but also in all directions each moment of each day.

From our different but not separate locations, Eldering is self-consciously participating as only the indivisible universe in the fundamental process in nature: cooperation for maturation.
*It has our physical bodies experience their lives as **consistently meaningful** rather than only going from one momentary physical pleasure to another.*

74

The following priorities are what Terry uses to double-check his physical body is behaving as a fully mature human being with the skill of human self-consciousness.

First, to be sure he has not slid into the immature behavior of acting as if he is "a separate part" instead of "a part of the indivisible universe," he becomes aware of everything existing within three-dimensionality to be sure he is enjoying the sensation of oneness as the container of all other experiences.
This has him more strongly experience the fundamental feelings of natural confidence, contented joy, and compassion than the relative feelings of mad, glad, sad, and scared.

Secondly, he double-checks to be sure his behavior in relationship to other human beings is fundamentally receptive.
If the universe operates as an indivisible whole, they are to him as his right arm is to his left arm, a part of himself.
Fundamentally, there is nothing to fear.
Thus, he chooses to always be receptive rather than reactive.

Thirdly, he becomes aware of which layer of maturity of the skill of human self-consciousness another is behaving as if it is the highest layer.

Fourthly, he makes sure he is identifying and executing loving ways to relate.
This is choosing Eldering behavior.

Fifthly, he is at all times listening for helpful information coming directly from the universe.

75

One of the patterns of behavior of our human being parts at the Teen layer can be interrupting others.

As an expression of individual free choice, it is giving priority to *immediately saying* the thoughts that come into their thinking.

This is not moving as one with the person or people they are with. When, at the appropriate time, it is pointed out interrupting is behaving as a first-class citizen and treating the other or others as second-class citizens, it usually immediately stops the interrupting. They realize this behavior gives the other or others no choice but to yield to it.

When they discover this is what they are doing, their highest priority of exercising individual free choice has them not want to be denying it to others, a response to the second half of maturation also occurring inside them at the Teen layer: sharing responsibility to give priority to the common good of the community.

In a group, oneness has us naturally oriented to consistently move in a consensual way and by consensual decisions.

It is moving as one, a local experience of oneness.

At the same time, we recognize the value of skillful leadership.

A skilled leader seeks consensual decisions of the group to sustain the experience of moving as one.

At the same time, they do not yield their responsibility to lead.

If a consensus decision on an issue cannot be achieved and the leader judges it is best to go in one direction, they lead the group in that direction.

A mature leader keeps the group informed of how it is going, continually and openly owns where it was wise and not wise, and also continually makes adjustments as a result.

They view this as part of their responsibility of *sustaining the mutual experience of consensus as the container of the group working together while allowing there to be seasoned leadership.*

The responsibility of the group is to choose leaders, or make sure the leaders who are appointed, have as one of their skills operating at this layer of maturity of leadership.

Oneness cannot be escaped, and there is only one oneness.

Mastering the skill of sustaining the experience of local oneness is part of the process of maturing into giving priority to the one and only oneness.

～ **76** ⌒

Personal growth activities, including psychotherapy, will also give priority to mastering the layers of maturity of the skill of human self-consciousness.

It will be the context within which all inner personal and interpersonal difficulties will be studied.

The days of identifying a problem and then a solution, or preferred behavior, and using effort, force, and discipline to make the change will be history.

Instead, the problem will be framed within the natural process of cooperation for health and maturation already occurring within the thinking of each human being.

By using mature free choice to identify relevant facts, and understanding them within the fact we are maturing your physical body up the layers of maturity of the skill of human self-consciousness, you can more easily identify the more mature behavior you want.

You can then allow the process of maturation inside you to naturally, effortlessly, freely, permanently, and without the need of effort, force, or discipline, to mature you into turning the more mature behavior you have identified using mature free choice into an inside belief in your thinking, a skill, and habit.
You let maturation do the work!
You only need to use mature free choice to identify facts.

Maturation is always a spiraling process where continuously less often will the old immature behavior choice emerge until it no longer emerges.

This is the maturation process of self-consciousness.

It allows you to continually use mature free choice to double check the accuracy of your choice until no longer necessary.

It is then fact-based knowledge in your thinking within your physical body (an inside belief), a skill to honor it, and eventually a habit.

The maturation is also permanent and the primary attention of your physical body is now free to focus on discovering and mastering the smaller skill of the next layer of maturity in the skill of human self-consciousness.

And then into the next more enjoyable skill of Eldering.

A few times it has been stated "from the inside you have sole and complete control of your physical body."

What is "the inside"?

Part of it is, when awake, the constant private conversation with yourself and, when sleeping, dreaming.

Where is it coming from?

If the indivisible universe is the only thing that is real, it has to be coming from it.

Using mature free choice to repeatedly study it reveals the private chatter is also coming through the layer of maturity in the skill of human self-consciousness at which you are operating.

At the Child layer, it is all about getting what you want.

At the Teen layer, it is all about exercising, and being respected as having the ability and right to exercise, individual free choice and care about the common good of the community.

At the Adult layer, it is expressions of your outside beliefs.

At the Elder layer, it is identifying in words the accurate relationships between the illusions of separate parts and words and the reality of oneness.

At the Mature Elder layer, it is solely about Eldering.

One of the ways you can double-check to see what layer of maturity you are operating on is to take a look at your private conversation with yourself.

It is the indivisible universe using its skill of human self-consciousness at your location for maturation.

It is primarily using it either at the layer of maturity you have accomplished and turned into a skill and habit or the next layer you are newly mastering.

Therefore, if you want to identify the layer at which you are operating, not where you think you are operating, as a personal scientist you can use mature free choice to repeatedly study your private conversation with yourself to see what it reveals as your layer of maturity or the one you are now mastering.

There is no escape from the oneness process of cooperation for maturation.

78

*Mature journalism will focus on the **fact** that what is primarily oc-curring in social interactions is mutually using mature free choice to forge consensus agreements on additional facts.*

Journalists will also see themselves as active participants in this natural process.
In the past, journalists have often seen themselves as separate from what is happening and then providing valuable information to the society and/or speaking truth to power in editorials.
The latter is based on the false assumption that desire for power and conflict are the fundamental processes in human society.
When immature, those can be the *priority actions of people.*
However, it is not the most fundamental process in nature or the self-consciously chosen process when human beings achieve full maturity in the skill of human self-consciousness.
To solely focus on the desire for power and the conflicts between and among people is to act as if they are the fundamental processes in nature.
It perpetuates those immature assumptions.

Mature journalists give priority to what they know is fundamentally occurring: cooperation for the health and maturation of human society by humans using mature free choice to identify additional facts so they eventually become freely chosen agreements all physical bodies will eventually honor.
Facts are the only things we can all eventually agree on.

Agreement is self-consciously moving as one.
When our local agreement is also moving as one with the reality of the oneness of nature, we are together operating at the high-est layer of maturity of the skill of human self-consciousness, the Mature Elder layer.
This is the continuous invention of self-consciously chosen agreements, based on facts, to guide our living together.
Mature journalists always give priority to identifying everything that is occurring as part of this fundamental cooperation for mat-uration process in human societies.

In fundamental physics, the latest most popular theory is the Holographic Theory, "holographic" representing three-dimensionality.

It is proposed as the answer to the "quantum entanglement," or "Einstein Dilemma," present in physics since 1927.

Basically, through a rather convoluted process, it assumes time and space, separate parts, are not real.

By default, the accurate assumption is the universe operates as an indivisible whole, the only other possibility.

This will eventually be discovered by all to be a fact, the most fundamental fact in physics.

However, it will not be discovered from a study of physics.
Physicists will discover it is a fact from the discovery of the importance of each person maturing to give priority to mature free choice. They will discover we are each first responsible for maturing into using mature free choice to achieve full maturity in the skill of human self-consciousness—being personal scientists—before we can be mature professional scientists.

We now know the facts:

The past and the future only exist in the mutually agreed upon illusions of words.

There is no beginning or end of the universe: time is not real.

Only oneness is real: separate places are also not real.

There is only cooperation for maturation in the Oneness Now.

It is all the past, present and future as one sensation.

It is real, and it is the only place that is real and we are it.

All thoughts in words about the past and future exist in the mutually agreed upon illusion of the Relative Now.

They are valuable illusion tools because they allow us to achieve full maturity in the skill of human self-consciousness.

In our human thinking, giving priority to what is real and second priority to valuable illusions is the way we equally value both rather than polarizing them as if they are separate parts.

The universe operates as an indivisible whole and all human beings are only the indivisible universe, the only thing that is real.

A positive result of the Covid-19 pandemic is for the first time in the history of Earth all the nearly 8 billion people were in the same conversation at the same time and feeling we are all in this together.

Just as anyone seeing the Earth from space can no longer assume the Earth is flat, no one in the future will be able to deny self-conscious human beings are, together, primarily responsible for, and able as a group, to manage Earth.

If we are to successfully manage it, we will have to agree on facts, the only things we can all agree on.

First, the most important fact our human being parts need to eventually agree on is the universe operates as an indivisible whole and, therefore, they are each only it, the only thing that is real.

The parts are different, they are not separate, and the self-conscious sensation of each of us being alive is the sensation of oneness: 3D.

The second most important fact we need to agree on is there are smaller skills of the layers of maturity of the skill of human self-consciousness, and human physical bodies must learn them in the natural progression.

Then we will know how to prioritize them.

Also, we must also mature to use mature free choice at the Elder layer to know these facts so remembering them is no longer in need of effort, force, or discipline.

The third most important fact to agree on is only Eldering in our thoughts and actions sustains within us the joy of the self-consciously known 3D sensation of oneness that confirms for us we are, indeed, giving priority in our thoughts and actions to Eldering.

This is the only way we will permanently succeed in managing together the environment of Earth and, yes, the rest of the universe, use a consensus building over time democratic process based of agreements on facts, have our economic activities give priority to cooperation for maturation, and operate everything else necessary for successfully managing our human lives together on Earth at the Mature Elder layer of maturity.

This is inevitable.

Cooperation for maturation cannot be escaped or stopped.

Democracy will also mature.
The next layer of maturity of it will be the emergence of agreement nations.
These are nations defined by an agreement rather than geography.

People want to primarily associate with people who share their worldview and work with them to mature their lives together and execute their Eldering activities.
The people who live in a town or rural area will have very different worldviews and traditions.
This easily locks them into a more competitive relationship with each other, the lowest level of cooperation.
Agreement nations provide an easier context to mature into primarily using compromise, agreement, and love.

They will not conflict with the geographically defined nations!
Quite the opposite; they will fully support them.
Agreement nation members will know they are necessary, vote in them, and be very active citizens of them.
While fully participating in both, their members will **give priority** to their agreement nation.
Local groups of friends who share a common worldview, such as Bernie Sanders Democratic Socialists, Tea Party Conservatives, Black Lives Matter Activists, Catholics, Buddhists, Islamists, or the Oprah Community, will form into a community of friends.

Like we think of nations, they will take full responsibility for the maturation, education, health, and life success of all their community members.

They will also join with other local communities that share the same worldview into an association of such communities.
Associations of these associations will also form.
This will allow all agreement nations to be transnational and grow to any size while, if successfully organized to do so, allowing the greatest power to remain with the individual, secondly with their community of friends, and thirdly with the agreement nation.

Probably, no community will be larger than 100 adults.

Each will elect two people to an association of communities.

There will not be more than 50 communities in an association.

Therefore, it will never have more than 100 people in its governing body.

Then, no association of associations will be more than 50 associations.

Two members will represent each association of associations so that governing body will also never have more than 100 people.

Regardless of how many communities around the world join, this pattern will continue.

Thus, before they vote people will never be in an election of more than 100 people where all can get to know each other.

For two reasons, the geographically defined nations will love the emergence of agreement nations.

First, they will be accepting full responsibility for the maturation and success of some of their citizens.

Secondly, they will be free research and development programs.

Anything they invent that works well, such as a better education or healthcare system, can be copied by the geographic nation.

With a successful example to point to, this will make it easier for all in the geographic nation to support its implementation.

Agreement nations will also be constantly forming, and reforming, based on a more comprehensive worldview and better strategies of operating for their members and the common good of all.

Because one can switch from one to another without changing one's residence, it will be easy for individuals, or communities, to leave one and joining another.

And different agreement nations will also make agreements with each other they find mutually wise.

Therefore, the next layer of maturity of democracy is the emergence of agreement nations.

This same pattern of organization can also be used to create Elder Bodies, mature people to guide the community and associations.

83

Since we now know there are layers of maturity of the skill of human self-consciousness, every mature organization will have an Elder Body.

Without regard for age, it will be a small group of people judged to be mature human beings and mature in the field that is the focus of the organization.

For instance, in a community of friends it will be the people judged to be mature human beings and mature in facilitation of meetings, building consensus agreements, and consistently stimulating a strong shared ownership of decisions by all.

The Elder Body will have the greatest power in the organization and be a self-perpetuating body.

This is because it is recognized they are best able to identify other mature human beings while allowing the organization to have members operating at different layers of maturity.

The second main responsibility of the Elder Body is to assist all in their maturation into full maturity in the skill of human self-consciousness.

The traditional Board of Directors, best renamed Board of Facilitators, is underneath the Elder Body.

It could be elected democratically by the members, be self-appointed and self-perpetuating, or created by the Elder Body.

If organizations are not comfortable with the Elder Body having the ultimate legal power, they could create an Elder Body as a committee of the Board of Directors.

It could have two members on the Board and serve the same role only without the veto power described in the next chapter.

As you will see, it is a veto power it is committed to never exercising except in extreme circumstances.

In the agreement nations, the Elder Bodies join in an association, and in associations of associations with the Elder Bodies of other communities, in the exact same way as the Boards of Facilitators.

At each layer of association, the Elder Body has the same agreement with the association Board of Facilitators described in the next chapter.

The Elder Body has three agreements with the Board of Facilitators:

1. It delegates full responsibility for running the organization to the Board of Facilitators,
2. It maintains the right to veto any decision made by the Board of Facilitators, and
3. It tries to never exercise its veto power.

Two members of the Elder Body are *ex officio* (without vote) members on the Board of Facilitators.
Otherwise, they fully participate in all the processes of the Board of Facilitators.
If they conclude there is a decision made, or about to be made, they are not certain is giving priority to cooperation for maturation, they can call for it to meet with the Elder Body for assistance.
The Elder Body facilitates the two groups into a consensus decision with terms all agree give priority to cooperation for maturation.
If not possible and an immediate decision is needed, there can be a decision by a 75% vote of the Elder Body.
If time is not an issue and if consensus cannot be reached in a meeting two weeks later, the 75% vote of the Elder Body will decide the issue.

The Elder Body will always give priority to doing all possible for the decision to be a genuine consensus decision of both groups before defaulting to a 75% vote of only the Elder Body.

When choosing new members of the Elder Body, it will go to great lengths to be sure there is widespread support for their choice, but it will make the final decision.

The Elder Body is the additional governance structure that both honors the fact there are layers of maturity of the skill of human self-consciousness and allows all involved the comfort of knowing the priority of the organization is self-conscious participation in cooperation for maturation, the fundamental process in nature (the universe).

Our economy will also mature.
What is fundamental in capitalism is not capitalist using capital to make more capital for capitalists.
That is secondary in importance.

What is primary in capitalism is honoring individual free choice and free markets.

This is honoring half of the Teen layer of maturity.
It is also why communist countries have allowed the emergence of private companies and free markets.
This is part of their maturation into honoring this half of the Teen layer of maturity within their societies.
Their governments have chosen to sustain giving priority to them maintaining strong parental control (Child layer).
The governments of the Western nations have chosen to give priority to individual free choice and democracy (Teen layer).
Both have their challenges of operating at a lower layer of maturity: paternalism in the first and, in the second, giving priority to individual free choice without also freely choosing to give priority to maturation based on agreement on facts, the second half.
As people in both societies mature into the mastery of the highest two layers of maturity of the skill of human self-consciousness, they will increasingly find ways to primarily cooperate with each other for the health and maturation of the indivisible universe. They will also work to assist their citizens to achieve full maturity in the skill of human self-consciousness, both eventually skipping the Adult layer.
The result will be strong support for transnational agreement nations where people are accepting full responsibility for Eldering their children and each other into full maturity in the skill of human self-consciousness; they will also meet their needs not provided by the geographically defined nations.
The transnational structure of agreement nations, and them being given priority by people, will also go a long way toward ending the polarizations that result in wars.

The emergence of agreement nations will also strongly support the emergence of common good capitalism, private sector activity in free markets that give priority to cooperation for maturation.

When human being participants in an economy have achieved full maturity in the skill of human self-consciousness, *the highest priority in their actions will always be cooperation with all the other participants for health and maturation.*

While continuing to honor individual free choice and free markets, all competitors in each product market—particularly where there are duopoly monopolies such as CVS-Walgreens or Home Depot-Lowes that are examples of very visible companies that control over 80% of their product markets in the US—will voluntarily meet with all in their product market and reach agreements that give priority to the common good, cooperation for maturation.

Appropriate government officials will be invited to attend.

Representing the citizenry, they can report the meetings were solely to reach agreements for the common good.

Then, like the teams in a sports league, they will voluntarily reach agreements that give priority to the common good (the rules for competition), such as a minimum wage that is a livable wage, healthy environment management policies, ending social injustice such as racism and sexism, and the amount they will annually contribute from profits to end poverty.

As a secondary activity, they will compete as ferociously as before, like the Los Angeles Lakers and the Boston Celtics.

The *priority* will no longer be the financial interests of the shareholders or any group of stakeholders.

The *priority* will be continuous voluntary cooperation for the health and maturation of the indivisible universe in a way that as best as possible for their time works for everyone involved.

Their agreements will also be continually maturing based on using mature free choice to agree on additional facts.

Eventually these more mature policies, voluntarily agreed to in the private sector, will be policies also chosen by the geographic nations.

Common good capitalism is the natural next layer of maturity of both honoring individual freedom and free markets and freely choosing to give priority to cooperation for maturation.

An honest global currency will eventually emergence.
Our current national currencies are a tax on low-income people.
Inflation is the equivalent of a tax on annual income.
People who live paycheck to paycheck, or close to it, pay this tax.
People who have assets invest them and part of their income from them pays this inflation tax.
Now that people are using credit cards more than cash, and with government officials again present, the credit card companies could meet, particularly if there is a crash of a national currency, to reach an agreement to instantly solve the problem.
As an improvement of their current currency, or the creation of a second national currency, they will agree on a new unit of measurement that can be used for transactions.

When your physical body knows it is only the indivisible universe, it does not take things personally.
All its fear and desire thoughts end.
All its thoughts of what others are thinking of it end.
They have nothing to do with Eldering, now the primary focus of its thoughts and actions.

Its skill of self-consciousness does not define who it is.
Your physical body is the indivisible universe using the tools of a human physical body part and self-consciousness for maturation.
Every perceived part is a tool of cooperation for maturation.

The parts are different, but they are not separate from one another.
Allow us to repeat that, like the parts within your skin, the parts are
different, but they are not separate from one another.

At full maturity in the skill of human self-consciousness, living is no longer primarily about your physical body and its relationship with other people or parts of the universe.
It is now primarily the enjoyment of the sensation of oneness and, secondly, the thoughts and actions of Eldering.
This is the only priority in your physical body's thoughts and actions that will have it consistently experience its life as meaningful.
We, the indivisible universe, always provides a "cooperation for maturation reason" to do one thing rather than another.

88

A trust fund will be created for every child at birth, either by the parents, employers, agreement nations, townships, geographic nations, or Trusts for All Children, a private organization recently created to eventually accomplish this.

Beginning on the child's eighteenth birthday there will be a monthly distribution until death.
It will provide minimum monthly financial security.

People will still be highly motivated to have greater income and be an active participant in cooperation for maturation.
However, the injustice of allowing poverty to exist on Earth will have been ended, with money now trickling up.
The Trust Funds for All Children, Inc. program makes it possible for ten family members and friends to contribute $11 a month for the first 20 years of a child's life that can result in the TFAC Trust Fund being $50,000 when the child is 20 years old, or larger if more donations. The money grows without taxation that has the monthly distributions be significantly higher than what is possible from other trust funds, and it could provide when elderly more than the average monthly US Social Security distribution.
In exchange for this, the remainder upon the death of the child goes into the TFAC Endowment Fund that invests it forever with any annual profits used to begin TFAC Trust Funds for poor children until every child is born with one.
Each day people can also make donations to the TFAC Now Fund that immediately uses them to create TFAC Trust Funds for poor children around the world.
These two funds could eventually end poverty on Earth.
How soon that happens solely depends on how many people around the world begin TFAC Trust Funds for their children and how much money is donated to the above two Funds.
It is also using the same route most who became wealthy, or wealthier, used to achieve it, by owning stocks.
For the last nearly 100 years, the US Stock market has provided an average annual return of 10.3%.
TFAC is using stock ownership to end poverty on Earth.
In a global capitalist marketplace, every child should be born with a trust fund that provides minimum monthly financial security.

Each year during the middle two weeks of October, people from all over the United States and beyond flock to New England to enjoy the colorful slow kaleidoscope of the leaves.

At different times, they change from primarily dark greens to limes to yellows to oranges to reds to browns and all colors together.

On the rolling hills, it is a gorgeous display of vibrating colors.

Nearly all think the leaves then fall off the trees.

That is another mutually agreed upon blind spot.

They do not fall off the trees; the colder weather expands the sap, and the leaves are pushed off the trees.

When your human physical body dies, it gets pushed off the tree of life and returns to the soil.

It has completed its participation in cooperation for the maturation of it all, and it is time for younger people to pick up the maturation process where your physical body left off.

If it has achieved full maturity in the skill of human self-consciousness, you know you were never your physical body, a thing defined by the illusions of times and places.

You are only the indivisible universe.

It is a wonderful time to have a beautiful and high fun party!

Terry remembers meeting the celebrated and respected nightly news anchor Walter Cronkite when he was in his eighties.

Unlike the very bright Melissa Lee of *Fast Money* or Jim Cramer of *Mad Money*, he could no longer find every word he wanted to say the moment he wanted to speak it.

He patiently waited for his slower moving sap to find it.

As you get older, like Walter Cronkite, it is important to know you are primarily the chooser and only secondly the doer.

You will understand the sap is moving slower in your tree of life.

You will then enjoy it as much as you enjoyed discovering sensations, feelings, the use of words, exercising individual free choice, choosing a worldview, using mature free choice to discover the fact the universe operates as an indivisible whole, accurately representing this in your thinking using the words you choose, enjoying the sensation of oneness, and Eldering.

Your death is then as much of a delight as those other phases.

You know you did your best each moment, and it could not have been anything less than your best; it was oneness maturing.

The above are just a few examples of the kinds of social maturations that will occur as more of our human physical bodies achieve full maturity in the skill of human self-consciousness.

Cooperation for maturation is the fundamental process in nature, and it cannot be escaped or stopped.
Therefore, the above, many more, and perhaps better maturations of these parts of our lives together, are inevitable.

Everything that is human is an agreement, a self-consciously moving as one with others or with all that exists.
If you and I agree to meet tomorrow at noon at Starbucks, can we point at the agreement with our fingers?
We can't; it is not a physical thing.
It only exists in our mutually agreed upon illusions of words.
They only exist within our mutually invented illusion the universe is separate parts.
It is these two valuable illusion tools that we, the indivisible universe, invented through our human being parts that has allowed them to mature to be self-conscious and then for two of them to agree to meet at Starbucks.

This is the most fundamental human process: facts and illusions co-operating for maturation.

The universe is an indivisible whole; that is a fact.
The assumption of separate parts and words are two mutually agreed upon illusions; they are also facts.
Cooperation between this reality and these illusions allows us, the indivisible universe, to be self-conscious at each of our different human being locations.
This is the process of *cooperation for maturation* between facts and illusions that allows for the skill of human self-consciousness in our human being parts of us, the indivisible universe.
Our human physical bodies are different, but they are not separate from each other, just as the physical parts within our human skins are different but not separate from each other.

91

Self-consciousness is a tool.
Everything other than the indivisible universe is a tool of it for maturation.
Our human physical bodies are also tools.
All thoughts about the parts as separate are tools.
Only thoughts about the different parts as secondary in importance to the reality of oneness are accurate thoughts.
This is the mature use of the tool of self-consciousness.

When we know we are only the indivisible universe, we do not take things personally.
All our fear and desire thoughts end.
All our thoughts of what others are thinking of us end.
They have nothing to do with Eldering, now the primary focus of our thoughts and actions.

Our skill of self-consciousness does not define who we are.
We are each only the indivisible universe using the tools of our human physical body and self-consciousness for maturation.
Every perceived part is a tool of cooperation for maturation.

The parts are different, but they are not separate from one another. Allow us to repeat that, like the parts within your skin, the parts are different, but they are not separate from one another.

At full maturity in the skill of human self-consciousness, living is no longer primarily about our physical body and its relationship with other people or parts of the universe.
It is now primarily the enjoyment of the sensation of oneness and, secondly, the thoughts and actions of Eldering.
This is the only priority in our thoughts and actions that will have us consistently experience our lives as meaningful.
It always provides a "cooperation for maturation reason" to do one thing rather than another.

We, the indivisible universe, is not the self-consciously known three-dimensional sensation of oneness.

We is not our relative sensations of hearing, smelling, tasting, seeing, and touching.

We is not our fundamental feelings of natural confidence, contented joy, and compassion.

We is not our relative feelings of some derivatives of mad, glad, sad, and scared.

We is not the assumption of separate parts and words that allow us to be self-conscious.

We is not our ability and right to exercise individual free choice.

We is not our outside beliefs.

We is not our ability and right to exercise mature free choice.

We is not our inside beliefs.

We is only Eldering.

However, your physical body can't consistently enjoy the self-consciously known sensation of oneness, and the fundamental feelings of natural confidence, contented joy, and compassion, until it has mastered the skill of human self-consciousness.

Only then will it know when it has given priority to the priority of one of the lower layers of maturity of it, an old habit, and correct that mistake by knowing how to return to giving priority to the primary skill of the highest layer, Eldering.

Also, it is the experience of the self-consciously known three-dimensional sensation of oneness in its physical body that reveals it is, indeed, Eldering.

When after making the mistake of sliding into giving priority to the activity of a lower layer priority and your physical body chooses Eldering again, that is also Eldering activity.

We, the indivisible universe, is the *activity* of cooperation for maturation.

Through human beings, we are doing it self-consciously.

At full maturity in the skill of human self-consciousness, your physical body is only Eldering.

In summary, there are two possible to be known and self-consciously experienced *fundamental sensations*: the illusory sensation of being only your physical body, "a separate part," and the real sensation of being "a part of the indivisible universe."

As part of the process of learning the words of a human language, our human physical bodies unconsciously assume they are each a separate part like each word is a separate part.

There are three dimensions of the skill of human self-consciousness: the assumption of separate parts, words, and oneness.

Until it discovers the importance of maturing into using mature free choice—the keeping of its power to choose and solely using it to repeatedly study its breathing to discover the universe operates as an indivisible whole, it is still operating as if the skill of human self-consciousness has only two dimensions: the assumption of separate parts and words.

Only when it has mastered the smaller skills of the first four or five layers using these two dimensions can it discover how to include the reality of the third dimension, oneness, and freely choose to give it priority over the other two.

The other two are equally valuable because they allow it to be a self-conscious part of the indivisible universe.

However, they are mutually agreed upon illusion tools we invented through our human parts that allow them to master the full skill of human self-consciousness.

When this is known, it naturally gives, *and also self-consciously freely chooses to give*, priority to the one that is real: oneness.

This has it realize it is living in three-dimensional reality and the sensation of being alive is the sensation of oneness, the sensation of the only thing that is real.

It is the enjoyable **real fundamental sensation** within which all relative sensations of hearing, seeing, smelling, tasting, and touching exist and now in its thinking are second in importance.

~ 94 ~

Here are the four smaller skills learned at the **Elder layer** where you make sure the words used by your human physical body, whatever words you choose, accurately represent in its thinking in words these most fundamental facts as inside beliefs:

1. Mature from giving priority to individual free choice to giving priority to mature free choice and using it to study its breathing by answering the ten questions to discover the universe operates as an indivisible whole.
2. Have its most fundamental inside belief be the most fundamental fact in physics: the universe operates as an indivisible whole.
3. Have its more mature self-definition be "I am first the indivisible universe that will not die and secondly my physical body that will die." And,
4. While fully doing both, give priority to the oneness pattern of thinking, prioritization, over the separate parts pattern of thinking, polarization.

There are also four smaller skills learned at the **Mature Elder** layer that are using the skill of human self-consciousness to master knowing the three-dimensional sensation of oneness:

1. Mature into experiencing everything occurring within three-dimensionality instead of two-dimensionality.
2. Realize your most mature self-definition is "I am *only* the indivisible universe, the only thing that is real."
3. Repeatedly use the words "There is no (your name)" to allow for the awareness of the direct experience of the sensation of oneness to emerge inside your physical body.
4. Since the universe is the only thing that is real, we discover the sensation of our physical body being alive is the sensation of oneness, the only fundamental sensation that is real.

This results in full maturity in the skill of human self-consciousness: the enjoyment of the sensation of oneness, the fundamental feelings of natural confidence, contented joy, and compassion, and the thinking and activity of Eldering.

95

Our physical body discovers there is only one priority *in its thinking and actions each moment* that sustains the joy of the sensation of oneness and, as a result, the enjoyable fundamental feelings of natural confidence, contented joy, and compassion.

It is Eldering.

Eldering is each moment giving priority to what it determines is its best action, large or small, of self-conscious participation in the fundamental process of nature, cooperation for the health and maturation of the indivisible universe.

As a complex skill, it cannot jump to mastering this skill.

It is only possible as the culmination of mastering in the natural sequence the smaller skills of the seven layers of maturity of the skill of human self-consciousness.

Only then has it *self-consciously mastered the skills of the lower layers* and can easily self-correct anytime it slides into giving priority to the priority of one of them, now old habits.

However, once these seven layers are known and your physical body has matured into the teen years, which is when its brain can master the last layers, it is not difficult to self-elder itself up the mastery of the smaller skills of the remaining layers.

Other people can be helpful, but only each human being can mature itself into the mastery of the skills of the last three layers.

They build on and must honor its ability and right to exercise individual free choice at the Teen layer.

In addition, only maturation into giving priority to exercising its ability and right of mature free choice will allow it to master the smaller skills of the last two layers of this skill, the most important skill for it to learn.

At full maturity in this skill and until death, the highest priority in its thinking and actions is Eldering.

It is the only thinking and actions that sustains the joy of the self-consciously known three-dimensional sensation of oneness and, as a result, the fundamental feelings of natural confidence, contented joy, and compassion as the container of all else it experiences.

This joy is only sustained by *knowing as an inside belief* it is only us, the indivisible universe, the only thing that is real.

96

As mentioned twice earlier, before 1492 most human beings did not observe the fact the Earth is round because they could not imagine a round as big as the Earth.

Today, most cannot observe the fact the universe operates as an indivisible whole in the same way they observe their physical bodies do because they cannot imagine an indivisible whole as big as the universe.

What also makes this difficult is the universe does not have an observable size: they can't step outside it and observe it.

Yet they easily observe all the parts within their physical bodies are cooperating for the health and maturation of them.

When they discover using mature free choice they are only the indivisible universe, the only thing that is real, they also easily observe all the parts within it are also cooperating for the health and maturation of what is now known as their entire physical body: reality is not a contradiction with cooperation the fundamental process within their skins and competition the fundamental process outside their skins.

They are now able to use mature free choice to confirm the Earth is round by observing a ship disappears from the bottom up when it sails out onto the sea and by seeing a picture of Earth from out in space.

Today they can also confirm the fact the universe operates as an indivisible whole by using mature free choice to answer the ten questions at the beginning of this book and observe it is obvious it is the indivisible universe that is naturally and effortlessly doing their breathing.

There will now be a widespread maturation by human beings into using mature free choice to study their breathing and observe the obvious fact we are all in this together as parts of one indivisible whole. Nearly all of humanity has mastered the first five layers of maturity of the skill of human self-consciousness and this means they are overly ready to master the last two layers.

This will eventually result in the maturation of all of humanity into the Elder and Mature Elder layers of maturity in the skill of human self-consciousness.

Cooperation for maturation cannot be escaped or stopped.

97

Your physical body now knows it is only the indivisible universe.
The parts of it are different, but they are not separate.
All it perceives as parts are primarily cooperating with each other
for maturation, the fundamental process in nature.

Its skill of self-consciousness is a skill.
Your physical body wants to master the full skill of it so it can correct its behavior any time it slides into old habits of giving priority to a lower layer of maturity of it, fundamentally the only mistake it can make.
It can then use this tool the same way it uses every other tool, solely to self-consciously participate in cooperation for maturation, the fundamental process in nature.
This is the skill of Eldering.

It is Eldering in its thoughts and actions that sustains in its physical body within your skin the self-consciously known three-dimensional sensation of oneness.
And it is this sensation of oneness in your physical body within your skin part of you that reveals it is Eldering in its thoughts and actions. At full maturity in the skill of human self-consciousness, your physical body is always enjoying the first, doing the second, and using mature free choice to double-check to be sure it is enjoying both.

One can't be happening without the other also happening.

98

The most important lesson Terry's physical body has learned during his life is to always give priority to Eldering.
And it is the experience of the self-consciously known three-dimensional sensation of oneness when doing it that reveals he is giving it priority in his thinking and actions.

He now knows why it took him into his seventies to learn it.
He had to mature up the seven layers of maturity of the skill of human self-consciousness in the natural progression and know their relationship of priorities to each other.
Until recent decades, he didn't know the following four things:
he had no idea there were higher layers of this skill, he was not able to skip the mastery of a layer, he did not know they build on one another, and he did not know he had to prioritize them in his thinking in the natural order he learned them.
Now that he knows these facts and is getting better at the mastery of the skills of all the layers and turning them into habits, he is keenly aware they are skills that can be taught and learned in the natural order before our children leave home and marry.
That did not happen for him and probably not for you either.
Our primary hope is what he has learned, and we have shared here through him, will be helpful to other human physical bodies in their self-eldering of them to full maturity in this skill.
We particularly hope this results in parents and educators discovering the importance of teaching our children this skill.

It is the most important skill for each human being to learn.

We also now know the day will come when all children on Earth will be Eldered into full maturity in this skill before they leave home, just as today they are all Eldered into knowing a human language, the Child layer of maturity of this skill.
Cooperation for maturation cannot be escaped or stopped.
Like giving priority in the spring to the Oneness Now when enjoying the beauty of a yellow daffodil popping up out of the ground and knowing it will grow and flower in the Relative Now, you can give priority to the Oneness Now and enjoy knowing in the Relative Now all of humanity will eventually achieve full maturity in the skill of human self-consciousness before they leave home, work closely with others, and marry.

Just as we know from repeated experience a daffodil will sprout leaves, a stem, and a yellow flower, we know from repeated experience rocks are hard, fire is hot, water runs downhill, and cherry tomatoes taste best when taken off the vine.

These are all cases where we used mature free choice and repeated experiences to identify facts.

By using mature free choice to repeatedly answer the ten questions at the beginning of this book each of our human being parts can now know the fact the universe operates as an indivisible whole.

It does so in the exact same way you experience the different parts within your skin cooperating for the health and maturation of your physical body.

And you also know facts are not contradictions.

Therefore, when you know the universe operates as an indivisible whole, what is a fact everywhere must also be a fact within your skin and between and among human beings."

You also know there is not a second thing to receive your power to choose.

By default, your only choice is to primarily use mature free choice to identify the facts you will use to guide your thinking.

From using mature free choice and repeatedly reviewing your experience of growing up, and observing your children growing up, it is also obvious the skill of human self-consciousness is a skill.

And like any complex skill, there are layers of maturity of smaller skills each of our human bodies must learn in the natural sequence to achieve full maturity in this skill.

From reading this book, you now know what Terry discovered they are and hopefully what you also, to some degree, discovered they are.

If you allow what he has discovered to only be a stimulus to you also using mature free choice to identify what you think they are, you will be using this book as someone who is maturing into mastering what he labeled the "Elder layer."

Here is a judgment with which we think you could now agree: over the next period all human beings will be maturing into mastering what Terry labeled the "Elder" and "Mature Elder" layers in the same way they have all matured into mastering the skills of the first five layers.

Your physical body is overly ready to do so.
It is overly ready to discover the sensation of being alive is the self-consciously known three-dimensional sensation of oneness.
Since maturation cannot be escaped or stopped, it is also inevitable this maturation will happen to all of humanity.

It will be the result of each day more human beings enjoying the fundamental fact in physics only oneness is real.

In the early 1970s, when Terry was thirty years old, he became friends with two men in their nineties, Ralph Barsodi and Scott Nearing.
During the Depression they both returned to self-sufficient home-steading in New England and wrote books about it.
Scott was a socialist, and Ralph was a libertarian.
Terry teased both by saying if they were on a deserted island and couldn't talk, they would organize their lives together in the exact same way.
At the end of an evening of Ralph giving a talk to friends at Terry's home, and only the two of them watching the fire in the fireplace burn down, there was a long pause and Terry knew Ralph was going to say something that would change his life.
Ralph finally spoke and said, "Just remember one thing. You can't ever protect anything from people."
Terry acted like it was profound, but he didn't know what it meant. He now does.
People can't behave at a higher layer of maturity than the one they are on.
Our naturally most important task is Eldering ourselves, our children, each other, and our organizations to full maturity in the skill of human self-consciousness.

Epilogue

Here are four programs, some already underway and some not, in which you could choose to participate:

Sensation of Oneness

This book is available both on Amazon (www.amazon.com/books) and Bookshop (www.bookshop.org) for $19.95. We encourage you to use the latter because it supports local bookstores. It can also be read free on our website so people around the world will have easy access to it. (If you buy a copy, thank you for financially supporting our educational program.)

The Sensation of Oneness website (www.sensationofoneness.org) will be the gathering place for people interested in mastering the skill of human self-consciousness. It will provide support for individual self-eldering activities and those who choose to create a study group. There will also be blogs and videos by Terry and others. It will assist your physical body in finding others in your geographic area interested in this. Hopefully, through the self-initiative of many, this Maturation Movement will grow and take many shapes, including an agreement nation.

It begins with each person accepting responsibility to self-elder their physical body to full maturity in this skill. The main purpose of this website is to assist you in this self-eldering process.

Sensation of Oneness Nation

If you are interested in being part of the agreement nation that is emerging based on the inside beliefs you have read, go to www.soonearth.org. We would love to have you either join ours or support you in creating an agreement nation with the worldview you choose. We will be happy to help you do the latter! We trust that agreement nations are the next layer of maturity of democracy and all agreement nations will eventually find ways to cooperate with each other for the health and maturation of us all.

We will only begin this community when enough people sign up on the website indicating they want to be involved in doing it, either in Western

Massachusetts (Amherst area) where I live or with a community of friends where they live or both simultaneously. This is not something Terry or anyone can do alone. He is now looking for people to join with him to create Sensation of Oneness Nation.

Come help us create this nation by agreement!

Common Good Capitalism Movement

If you are interested in being part of building the Common Good Capitalism Movement, go to www.commongoodcapitalism.org. Common good capitalism is already happening. The purpose of this movement is to speed it up.

Trust Funds for All Children

If you would like to create a trust fund for a child you love, as described in this book and regardless of where you live on Earth, we have created Trust Funds for All Children, Inc. (TFAC), www.tfac.earth. It is an easy way anyone can begin a trust fund for a child they love—your child, a grandchild, or a friend's child—by having a few friends by electronic transfer (one decision) contribute $11 a month for the first 20 years of the child's life ($132 a year). Plus, the creation of it, by even a few people, makes it easy for family members and friends to make additional contributes to it on birthdays, holidays, graduations, and from people's wills. And parents and grandparents who can afford it can begin one at the birth of a child with significant capital. Financial planners can also encourage the latter.

A TFAC Trust Fund will provide a monthly distribution to the child beginning on their 18th birthday until death. It can be spent anyway the child, now an adult, chooses. The distributions will be larger than possible from other trust funds because it is part of the Pooled Income Fund program of the IRS. This allows the money in it to grow without taxation for the entire life of the child. In exchange for this benefit, upon death the remainder goes into the TFAC Endowment Fund. The money in it is invested forever in the stock market and only any annual profits are used to begin TFAC Trust Funds for poor children. There is also the TFAC Now Fund. Any money contributed to it is immediately used to create TFAC Trust Funds for poor children around the world. Along with consistently helping parents create TFAC Trust Funds for their children, TFAC will have a strong on-going fundraising campaign to bring donations into these two Funds until every child on Earth is born with a TFAC Trust Fund.

Check out our website to learn more, www.tfac.earth. And both set up a TFAC Trust Fund for your children or grandchildren and encourage all parents and grandparents you know to do it for their children or grandchildren.

Companies can commit to provide an additional employee benefit of taking three to five of the ten $11 monthly contributions for the children of employees. We believe employers providing this incentive will be the primary way TFAC Trust Funds will be created for more and more children each year.

And all will soon know this is both best for the child and best for permanently ending poverty on Earth.

Two Other Items That May Be of Interest to You

An Easy Way to Lose Weight

Throughout my life I have tried many ways to lose weight. (Being on the board of Ben & Jerry's for eighteen years didn't help!) Many of us in developed nations have easily gained more weight than we like. Here is what I have discovered is, for Lucy and me, an easy way to lose weight. It is a combination of intermittent fasting and protein drinks.

Intermittent fasting works because when you haven't eaten for eighteen hours, the last hours your body takes what it needs from your stored fat. Eighteen hours, or an hour or two more or less as you choose, is best. The protein drink below makes it easy to do.

To lose weight each day, Lucy and I don't eat until after 10am in the morning. Then stop eating by 4pm. (You can also eat between noon and 6pm, but I think it good to have a hardy breakfast.) We have a full organic meal at 10am: meat, vegetables, and a desert of fresh fruit salad. (It is important to have much protein at this meal to reduce the loss of muscle mass.) Then, before 4pm, we have a protein drink with milk or almond milk. I use *Garden of Life* Raw Organic Meal (20g protein). I love it because I don't feel hungry until I go to bed. We add greens (organic kale, spinach, and others to it) that we blended in a blender earlier (we call this "green drink"). That gives us eighteen hours of not eating.

The other actions to monitor are to not eat a lot at your morning meal or snacking a lot, especially on fattening foods. We try to eat very little between breakfast and taking the protein drink. Also, drink plenty of water when not eating. And tea and coffee are fine any time. And a spoon or two of ice cream, not a bowl of it, is also fine. Finally, get exercise to keep your muscles toned. I do 100 crunches and 25 pushups in the morning and take walks.

Be comfortable with what I call "Cheat Days!" For instances, when I go out to dinner with my daughter, I just call it a "Cheat Day!" and go back on the above the next day.

Doing this, I have recently lost 32 pounds in a few months. Sadly, when I recently went to a conference for a week, I put eight pounds back on (and I truly enjoyed eating all the great foods available!). When I got home, I just went back on it and took them off again. (And I love how delicious breakfast tastes when I haven't eaten for eighteen hours!)

Investing to Make the World a Better Place

Eleven years ago, two friends and I created **Stakeholders Capital, Inc.,** a socially responsible asset management firm with offices in Amherst, MA and Santa Monica, CA. Fortunately, socially responsible investing has gone mainstream. It is now widely understood you do not give up financial performance, and can have even better financial performance, by only investing in companies that are making the world a better place for us all.

At **Stakeholders Capital** we specialize in also providing socially responsible private placements in, for instance, solar and organic farming companies, that provide a strong financial as well as social return.

You don't have to live near one of our offices. We have clients around the country. If you want to invest socially responsibly, give our CEO, Andrew Bellak, a call at 413-306-3244.

Rose On the Cover

The rose on the cover is what my father, Hienie Mollner, would draw beneath his name each time he signed a note or card with a gift. He would also add it beneath his hand-written magic marker signs on butcher paper for the sausage, such as jaternices, he wanted to make sure he sold that day. He would misspell jaternice on purpose. He would then post it in a prominent place on the wall behind his meat cutting block in Mollners Meat Market he ran with his two brothers, Emerick and Leo, in the Austian-Hungarian community in Omaha, Nebraska. When a customer would point out the misspelling, he would act like he couldn't believe he had done that. He would then say, "Hey! Would you like some jaternices?" They would usually respond, "Sure Hienie, give me a couple jaternices."

When a customer asked him what the rose meant, he would say, "That rose is always watching to be sure you are following your conscience." It was the words he used that in his way was honoring the oneness of nature.

For him, the three leaves represented the Father, Son, and Holy Spirit in his Catholic tradition. For me they represent the three dimensions of the skill of human self-consciousness: the assumption of separate parts, words, and oneness (in the language of science, time, space, and oneness).

Since nothing was written down for many decades, for all we know the following may have been the original meaning since it now represents what we now know are facts.

Metaphorically, the Father represents oneness, the only thing that is real. The Son represented the skill of self-consciousness based on the mutually agreed upon illusion tools we invented of the assumption of separate parts and words used to master the first five layers of human maturation. And the Holy Spirit represented the use of mature free choice to discover the fact the universe is an indivisible whole and the last two layers of human maturation. We then identify ourselves as first the universe that will not die and only secondly our physical bodies that will die. We eventually discover the sensation of being alive is the sensation of oneness, the sensation of being the only thing that is real. This is the achievement of full maturity in the skill of human self-consciousness. The Holy Spirit is the most fundamental cooperation for maturation between reality (oneness) and illusions (separate parts and words), the fundamental process in human self-consciousness.

This is pure speculation! There was no one back then with an iPhone recording what they were thinking and saying, but it is fun speculation that this was what they were thinking. It represents the facts they could have discovered, and in their own way probably did discover. However, they probably lacked the understanding we now have of the relationship between the oneness of nature and human words. That made it difficult to communicate it in a way that would last for thousands of years without projections into it from people operating at one of the lower layers of maturity as if it is the highest layer.

Fortunately, we do not need to be concerned about the past or future. They only exist in the mutually agreed upon illusions of words. We only need to make sure we are using mature free choice to study our breathing to identify the most fundamental fact the universe operates as an indivisible whole. Then also use it to identify additional important facts, especially those that define each layer of maturity of the skill of human self-consciousness. Then by consensus we can build our lives together based on agreement on facts and the maturation of ourselves, our children, and everyone else into full maturity in the skill of human self-consciousness. It is the solution to all defined as a problem.

∿ About the Author ∿
Terry Mollner, Ed.D.

In the 1970s he was one of the earliest pioneers of socially responsible investing, what is today referred to as ESG investing (environment, social, and governance), responsible investing, and impact investing. With his friend Robert Swann, they created the Institute for Community Economics (ICE). Once a month during the late 1970s, and over more than a year of meetings, Dr. Mollner guided fifteen social activist leaders from around the country in the writing of one of the first set of social screens for investing. With Wayne Silby, one of those leaders, those screens were used to establish the Calvert Funds (www.calvert.com), the first family of socially responsible mutual funds. Today it is one of the largest with over $33 billion under management.

The team at ICE also created one of the first "community development financial institutions (CDFIs)." There are now over 1100 CDFIs in communities throughout the USA and are now also supported with annual grants and loans from the US Treasury Department. Today CDFIs make loans to low-income housing projects, social and cooperative enterprises in low-income communities, and microloan programs (small uncollateralized business loans) around the world.

In the early 1990s, this had Dr. Mollner take the lead to create the Calvert foundation, Calvert Impact Capital (www.calvertimpactcapital.org). It raised low interest and uncollateralized capital from investors to fund this industry and to make loans to reduce poverty around the world. It has raised and loaned over $3 billion and is one of the largest contributors of private capital to the growth of this movement.

In 2000, he stepped up to assist Ben & Jerry's (www.benjerry.com) in its need to be bought by a multinational to deal with its distribution requirements as it was becoming a global brand. As part of its purchase by Unilever, he and the board arranged for a contract that allowed Ben & Jerry's to both continue to operate as an independent company with a self-perpetuating board of directors and have a contract that obligated Unilever to allow it to continue forever to spend the same percentage of its annual budget on social activism as of the year it was bought. It could also take any position on a social issue without seeking the approval of Unilever. Ben & Jerry's is the only socially responsible company bought by a multinational to sign such a contract. Terry has recently resigned from the boards of the Calvert Funds, Calvert Impact Capital, and Ben & Jerry's to focus on building the Maturation Movement.

Dr. Mollner is also a founder and chair of Stakeholders Capital (www.stakeholderscapital.com), a socially responsible asset management firm with offices in Massachusetts and California. Since 1973 he has been the founder and executive director of Trusteeship Institute, recently re-named Trust Funds for All Children (www.tfac.earth). In the 1980s, it was best known for introducing the Mondragon Cooperatives to Americans. Dr. Mollner described them at conferences around the United States and, at the invitation of the Reagan White House, to members of his admin-istration and members of Congress. In the 1980s, the stimulus of that meeting played a significant role in Congress launching the Employee Stock Ownership Program (ESOPs) that has assisted millions of Americans to have ownership of stock in the companies in which they work.

He is a co-founder of three communities of friends, all of which to dif-ferent degrees still exist after nearly forty years, and the author of several other books including *Common Good Nation, Common Good Capitalism Is Inevitable, Our Mutual Blind Spot,* and soon *Mature Free Choice.*

Made in the USA
Middletown, DE
08 February 2022

59913987R10086